# THE EMBODIED SELF

# THE EMBODIED SELF

## Movement and Psychoanalysis

*Katya Bloom*

KARNAC
LONDON    NEW YORK

First published in 2006 by
H. Karnac (Books) Ltd.
6 Pembroke Buildings, London NW10 6RE

British Library Cataloguing in Publication Data

A C.I.P. for this book is available from the British Library

ISBN-10: 1 85575 394 4
ISBN-13: 978 1 85575 394 5

Edited, designed and produced by The Studio Publishing Services Ltd,
www.publishingservicesuk.co.uk
e-mail: studio@publishingservices.co.uk

Printed in Great Britain

10 9 8 7 6 5 4 3 2 1

www.karnacbooks.com

# CONTENTS

*ACKNOWLEDGEMENTS*

I would like, first of all, to thank, Carole Satyamurti and Anne Alvarez, whose supervision was invaluable throughout the journey toward completion of my PhD from which this book has been developed. I also wish to thank Michael Rustin, Margaret Rustin, Andrew Cooper, Karl Figlio, and Biddy Youell, all of whom supported this project and made valuable suggestions. Maria Rhode also supported my interest in the interface between movement and psychoanalysis by supervising the writing of an earlier article on the subject. Carola Gross, Sara Bannerman Haig, Harry Blumenthal, Emer Heavey and Katya Benjamin each read parts of the manuscript and gave me valuable feedback.

I am also indebted to numerous movement teachers and colleagues who have helped me to develop this work. In particular, I am grateful to Irmgard Bartenieff, who encouraged me to attend the certificate programme at the Laban/Bartenieff Institute of Movement Studies in New York in 1980, and thus set me on a particular course of inquiry and professional development; and Suprapto Suryodarmo, whose teaching continues to deepen my appreciation of what can be experienced through embodied movement, more than I could have ever anticipated. Eleanor Goff, Ruth Noble, Janet

Bungener, Rolene Szur, and Jonathan Bradley also supported my development of the ideas in this book in various essential ways. Perhaps the greatest integration of learning has come through working with students and with patients. I am especially grateful to those who have given me permission to include material from our work together.

My husband, Hugh Kelly, has offered his unwavering support, both emotional and practical, including giving me invaluable feedback on the manuscript. Our stimulating and creative discussions have added spice to my life and have filtered into this work in sometimes unpredictable ways; not to mention his patient computer competence, which was a godsend on more than one occasion.

Parts of the material from Chapters Five and Ten were first published in 2000, in *Free Associations*, 8(46). My grateful thanks to Vera Maletic and Moulton de Gruyter, publishers, for permission to reproduce the drawings in Chapter Two, originally published in *Body, Space, Expression,* where Kimberly Elam adapted the drawings from Laban's *Choreographie.* And thanks to Roz Carroll for permission to refer in Chapters Three and Four to material of hers that is currently unpublished.

Last, but by no means least, thanks to the diligent team at Karnac for supporting this project and bringing it to fruition.

# ABOUT THE AUTHOR

**Katya Bloom, PhD**, is a movement psychotherapist in private practice in London. She taught on the Dance Movement Therapy training at the University of Surrey Roehampton from its inception in 1985 until 2002. She is a Certified Movement Analyst from the Laban/Bartenieff Institute of Movement Studies in New York, and is a qualified teacher of Suprapto Suryodarmo's Amerta Movement. She also teaches movement to actors at the Royal Academy of Dramatic Art, and is the author of two stage plays. She is co-author with Rosa Shreeves of *Moves: A Sourcebook of Ideas for Body Awareness and Creative Movement* (1998). She has pursued her interest in the interrelationships between psychoanalysis and movement since coming to London from the USA in 1983, culminating in her PhD, "Movement as a Psychophysical Process", under the auspices of the University of East London and the Tavistock Clinic, in 2005.

*To Hugh*

*Anne Alvarez*

In this original and exciting book, the author has created a bridge between two quite different disciplines and managed to treat both with respect, while firmly showing both what each could learn from the other. More than that, her detailed observations of babies, children, and her adult patients reveal a real and creative integration of the two viewpoints. She argues her case so clearly and so eloquently that I shall just pick a few points that are particularly illuminating.

### *What movement theory and therapy can give to psychoanalysis*

As Katya Bloom herself points out, psychoanalysis has never ignored the body. Freud, after all, said that the ego was first and foremost a body ego, and made us aware from the start of the significance in human nature of unconscious preoccupations and fantasies about the sexuality of our parents' bodies. Klein went on to stress the importance of fantasies about the mother's feeding breast, and she and her followers showed how deep infantile parts of the personality could be constantly relating to bodily features of the parents: the breast, vagina, and the father's penis were all given prominence in this early thinking. Later, the work of Bion, with its emphasis on our inborn expectation of meeting a human being with a mind, moved our attention up to the rather neglected area above the neck. Bloom, like the analysts, deplores the Cartesian tendency to split the mind from the body, but she goes further in her insistence on three things: first, attention to the whole body; second, attention, as her title indicates, to the body of the self, not only to fantasies about the body of the parents; third, to the crucial issue of the body *in movement*.

Central to her thinking is the concept of the movement of one body in relation to another, or—within the body—of the way in which different parts of the self relate to each other. My own view is that the study of movement restores a dynamic quality to the somewhat static geographization of the mentalization of mother's body parts, as seen in some psychoanalytic work in the past. Bion said that thoughts interacted with each other in dynamic, almost physical ways, and often quite independently of the thinker. Bloom insists on the importance of flow, or the lack of it; that is, the way in which recurring patterns of recalcitrance can lead to permanent blocks in flow. These ideas are not inconsistent with modern psychoanalytic study of the minute tos and fros in the transference and countertransference, but Bloom's emphasis on observing what may be happening within and to the patient's body and the way it moves or fails to move might enrich the work even with a patient who is lying apparently immobile on the couch It is likely to be particularly important with psychosomatic patients, for example. Her experience in naturalistic infant observation as taught by Esther Bick has hugely enriched her repertoire, and although it may be that child psychotherapists can be expected to notice a good deal about the child's movements because children are always on the move, I can imagine that they, as well as the adult therapists and psychoanalyts, could learn much from the way the language of movement theory analyses types of movement and types of posture. It makes us attend to that which might be only half grasped in our patients as well as in out own somatic countertransference.

## What can psychoanalysis give to movement therapists?

*A two person psychology, the signifance of fantasy, and the importance of the therapist's countertransference*

Modern psychoanalysis involves a two- (really three-) person psychology. The self is not seen in isolation: its relation to other people in the external world, especially to imagined figures in the inner world, are very much the subject of study. No function, even that of intelligence is seen as entirely separate from our relationship to internal others or as understandable without those relationships. But an even older tradition in psychoanalysis is the study of fantasies, conscious and unconscious, which underlie all our reactions and behaviours, even the most rational. A few years ago I became interested in how children's walking often seemed driven by particular unconscious fantasies that also appeared in their drawings or dreams and in the transference. One boy, Peter, was always falling over because, it seemed, he was in such a hurry that he leaned over beyond his centre of gravity. He was indeed, a very impatient little boy, but there was more to it. We began to notice how tentative he was in his relationships and in the transference, and how difficult he found it to say a clear "yes" or "no"—to "put his foot down", as it were, or "stand his ground". He had an image inside of a much loved but fragile mother. One day he had a dream that he was flying above the earth, wanting to land. But he did not dare to land because the ground was covered with beautiful white flowers, and he realized that his landing would crush them. This was exactly his dilemma, and as, over the years, his fantasied mother was seen as stronger, so he too became more upright and stronger, and the falling ceased.

Alan, another boy, was overweight and walked, spoke, and thought in a terribly wooden way. He was very bad at sports, even finding ordinary school walks a terrible effort, and, as a result, was very much the butt of his schoolmates' mockery. Eventually, after some years of treatment, he took up ice hockey. It seemed a crazy thing to do, because he suffered agonies of terror of being knocked over—which happens all the time in that game! But we learned together that, although he was still very awkward and slow, he loved the *idea* of being able to slide smoothly over the ice, and this seemed to represent ideal fantasies both about himself and his object. He longed to feel safe enough (and he somewhere knew that he needed to feel ordinary enough), to let go and to move forward in his emotions, his thoughts, and in his life. The smoothness of the ice seemed to stand for a frictionless, lubricated object that would, in a sense, let go enough for him to move on, pass it by, grow up, and yet still be available to support him. (This is what every toddler needs as he learns to walk upright, and Bloom's book has much to say on this subject.) I had to watch my countertransference very carefully in order not to get drawn in to the mutually blocking arguments he was so fond of.

Why do, for example, great athletes and great dancers make their runs, leaps and glides seem so effortless and beautiful? Is it only a question of muscles and training? Will a one-person psychology do to explain this, or do we need a two-person psychology? Is it also partly because such people seem to experience (and almost to make) the earth underneath smoother, less resistant, softer and more resilient, and to experience the very air, space, and heights around them as something inviting, accessible, and smoothly scaleable? John Lahr wrote that the great tapdancer, Savion Glover, seemed to be "playing the floor", and Glover agreed that he was "feeling the stage for sounds". My patients described above unfortunately stood and moved on a much more recalcitrant planet, but it was important for them and for me to understand the precise nature of their fantasies concerning the fragilities and perils of the ground beneath. I wish Bloom's work had been available to me at the time. Meanwhile, I think dance and movement therapists, will, in their turn, gain much from Bloom's weaving of their work together with the psychoanalytic study of object relations, of the manner in which defences develop, and of the fantasies and feelings that shape all these things from infancy on.

# PREFACE

In setting out to write about the interrelationships between the body and the psyche, and explore links between the articulation of the body in movement and the articulation of thoughts in words, I follow all those who have attempted the challenging feat of putting into words what is essentially non-verbal.

For more than thirty years, as a dancer/choreographer, teacher, therapist (in that order), I have explored from various angles how bodies both give form to experience and are the site for recognition of what is communicated by others. I am particularly interested in the choreography of primitive communications between infants and their carers, and how these lay the baseline for psychophysical patterns in later life. This interest has been at the heart of my work as a movement psychotherapist.

In setting out to read this book and *embody* the body–mind interface I'm exploring, the reader may have to consider how to read with their whole body, to give what I call their *embodied attentiveness* to both the theory in Part I and the observational and clinical material in Parts II and III. One example of a challenge I found myself faced with was how to convey to the reader that in this context a word like *recognition* implies a bodily experience as well as a mental one.

In exploring ways of extending the quality of my own *embodied attentiveness* in clinical work, I always give time for settling into my own skin, as it were, before a patient arrives; but more recently, I have been giving time for experiencing my body in movement after a patient leaves. I have found that this *in-forms* me about what part of the patient has been left behind, disowned for whatever reason and projected into and absorbed by me. It facilitates the process of hypothesis building as a therapist.

Through the continuing development of my work in this way, I feel the purpose of the book—to integrate psychoanalytic object relations theory and experiential movement analysis—has come vividly to life. I am often amazed by the clarity with which an internal figure, which could be described as either a part of the patient or a version of another figure they carry in their internal world, can sometimes seem to crystallize in me through movement.

Embodying these character-like figures, discovered through and informed by movement, makes a natural link with the other direction my work has taken—as a teacher of movement for actors at the Royal Academy of Dramatic Art. Although this book mainly aims to foster the integration of movement and psychoanalytic thinking within various kinds of psychotherapy relationships, I have included a small section on my work with actors, whose business it also is to authentically experience psychological and emotional states and convey the complexity of the human psyche.

What is it to be embodied? And why choose movement as the focus of my attention? Embodiment is another way of describing the integration of parts—mind, body, feelings, internal and external worlds. Movement is a medium that gives form to, and can monitor changes in, what is occurring (often unconsciously) from moment to moment. Movement takes place in present time and space, but is informed by both past history and future hopes.

In drawing together psychoanalysis and psychotherapy on the one hand and movement analysis and movement psychotherapy on the other, I am implicitly suggesting that each side could benefit by insights offered by the other. I hope that readers from both sides may approach this exploration with curious and open minds. Each may feel confronted by "jargon" from the other side—the language of "object relations" from psychoanalysis and the language of "Effort theory" from movement analysis initially can seem foreign and unnecessarily abstract. I have done my best to make the languages accessible and to draw links between them. My own fascination and motivation has been to digest and embody both sets of theory, derive meaning from their interrelationships, and apply them within my work.

I have taken steps to preserve the anonymity of all the people whose material is used in the book. I wish to point out that I have used the term "patient" to refer to the people I work with, rather than calling them "clients", which is more normal in movement psychotherapy. I attribute this decision to having heard psychoanalyst Nina Coltart discuss this question many years ago—did she work with patients or clients? Her feeling was that a patient is someone who (at least on some level) acknowledges a need for help; whereas a "client" can gloss over this essential starting point. The use of the term patient, therefore, is a mark of respect for the journey embarked upon in therapy.

# PART I
# OVERVIEW AND THEORY

# CHAPTER ONE

# Laying the groundwork

"He that has eyes to see and ears to hear may convince himself that no mortal can keep a secret. If his lips are silent, he chatters with his finger-tips; betrayal oozes out of him at every pore"

(Freud, 1905e)

My intention in this book is to examine the interrelationships between the body and its movement and psychic and emotional states. I am a movement psychotherapist[1] in private practice, and I have also been a dancer, movement analyst, and a teacher of movement as a source of self understanding, personal expression, and non-verbal communication for over thirty years. For much of that time I have also been a student of psychoanalytic thinking.

The two disciplines—movement and psychoanalysis—have represented two sides of a coin in my experience, in the same way that body and mind can be said to be reflections of each other. Yet, often their interconnections have not constituted an easily describable one-to-one relationship, a comfortable fit between body and mind. This book comes out of a strong wish to puzzle over and grapple with the complex ways in which the two disciplines inter-sect and inform each other. The writing of this book is a process that has its roots, therefore, in two kinds of articulation, that of the body in movement, and that of the mind in thought.

My overarching aim is to explore how useful links can be made between the two disciplines. How can we gain access to the psyche (by which I mean both mental and emotional processes) via the body? I will be considering whether, when taken together within the context of therapeutic relationships, the interplay of the two may provide greater possibilities for deriving insight from patients' material than either discipline could when focused on alone.

Specifically, I will be asking the following questions:

- What can psychoanalytic theory contribute to the perception and understanding of emotional and psychological processes that may enhance and help to underpin the theoretical foundations in the profession of dance movement therapy? What elements of psychoanalytic theory are most relevant for this exploration?

- Conversely, can closer attention to movement, supported by some experience of both movement analysis and the practice of movement, offer an added dimension of insight into emotional and psychic processes, which could be of use to psychotherapists, psychoanalysts and psychoanalytic observers? What elements of the language of movement are most relevant for this exploration?

## Preverbal language

The nature of the relationship between an infant and its primary caregivers underlies the development of the psyche throughout later life. Even the primordial memory of intra-uterine life has been shown to affect both body and psyche after birth, "especially if pre-natal events are reinforced by post-natal experiences" (Piontelli, 1992, p. 1). Joyce McDougall suggests that "the early transactions between mother and nursling may together determine the tendency to somatic rather than psychological reactions to internal and external stress" (1995, p. 153).

The tensions that an infant feels if its needs, for whatever reason, go unmet, register not only as physical experiences; they are intertwined and confused with emotional experiences. As child psychotherapists have learned from their patients, physical tensions may cover attempts to cope with terrifying infantile fears—of annihilation, of falling to pieces, of melting, of dissolving, etc. The infant will do its best to rid itself of these powerful tensions by a number of different means, which have been collectively described by Esther Bick as ways of creating a "second skin" (Bick, 1968). I will explore Bick's work further in Chapter Three, but suffice it to say here that I am interested in exploring how these primitive patterns of defence become embedded, and can endure long beyond childhood.

In part, I am investigating whether attention to the body and its movement can provide a medium closely related to the infant's preverbal language, through which the primitive phantasies and "second skin formations", can be touched upon, so to speak, and brought into consciousness where they can be thought about and tolerated. Can attention to the body and movement offer a route by which primitive feelings and parts of the self that may have been split off and dissociated from can be retrieved? If parts of the psyche become somatized and lodged in the musculature, or projected outwards into another person, can movement offer a means of recovering and reintegrating them? Winnicott wrote of "the psyche indwelling in the soma" (1960, p. 45). Can a synthesis of the perspectives of psychoanalysis and movement analysis provide a helpful route towards working through the impediments to restoring this "indwelling"? Can anxiety and depression, for example, be explored as psychophysical phenomena?

## Interweaving two languages

By *embodiment*, I mean the tendency towards a balance and integration of the different aspects of the self—sensory, emotional, and mental—within the containing confines of the bodily structure, bounded by the skin and responsive to internal and external stimuli. *Movement*, in this context, refers to bodily responses to these stimuli; it comprises posture, gesture, position as well as movement through space. The felt sense in stillness, including physical or psychic restrictions, is also part of movement. It is not only about what one *does*, but is also a sensorial registering of who and how one *is*. I am interested in what insights can be gained through paying attention to the subtleties of this non-verbal realm, and in how it informs and interacts with thoughts and words.

I wish to make clear that movement is my primary "language" in this enquiry. I am not a psychoanalytic clinician. I have drawn on elements of psychoanalysis that link with and add meaning to my embodied experience. Broadly speaking, it seems to be the area of *feeling* that can be said to belong to both disciplines equally. What the two perspectives seem to me to share are an interest in the relationships between the internal and the external worlds, and between self and other; and, even though the languages are distinctly different, both respect free-associative articulation of one's moment-to-moment experience. Neither domain has a monopoly on feeling, and it is also clearly acknowledged that both words and movement can be used quite effectively to *avoid* feelings as well as to express or embody them. In psychoanalysis it is sometimes observed that *action* is used as a means of escape, replacing thinking with "acting out" or repressing feelings (Tustin, 1990, p. 152). This, though true, does not take into account that the body and its movement may also provide a powerful means of making contact with deep layers of the self, and may be particularly suited to rediscovering and reworking preverbal patterns.

In developmental terms, the non-verbal realm of expression is the first to exist, and therefore can be said to underlie the emergence of patterns of thought. From the beginning of psychoanalysis Freud proposed that bodily experience, derived from physical sensation, constitutes the first experience of a sense of self. It is clear that the "bodily ego" is not only "first and foremost" as he famously wrote in 1923b, but it lays the baseline for development throughout life; and that it is, in fact, crucial for the bodily ego to be involved in any real transformation. Psychoanalyst Henri Rey wrote, "I have become more and more convinced that in every analysis one has to arrive at the body–self if one wants to achieve deep and enduring change" (1994, p. 267). Resnick (2001, p. 90) reminds us that, as early as 1913, "Scheler referred to an initial stage of pre-communication characterized in particular by the role that the body plays: the most primitive of intentions are revealed by the body". Therefore, it stands to reason that an interweaving of psychoanalytic principles with a therapeutic method that brings the body, its movement, its sensations, and the recognition of emotional affect within the body into the foreground may prove fruitful for both disciplines.

## Countertransference

I am interested in thinking not only about the effect for patients of being more in touch with their psychophysical experience, but also the effect for the clinician of being able to experience, as Allen Shore (2001) describes it, that "the body is the tool for psychic attunement". In other words, the therapist's own bodily sensations can provide a deepening of empathic connection with the patient through a more consciously embodied awareness of the manifestations of the transference and the countertransference.

What Freud (1912e) referred to as "evenly suspended attention" and Bion (1962) called "capacity for reverie" describe a state of spaciousness of mind, a state of multi-dimensional receptivity to the moment-to-moment experience of what is happening, without being pulled into the past or future of "memory or desire" (Bion, 1967). I wonder whether this capacity might imply and depend on the therapist's (conscious or unconscious) sense of three-dimensional embodied presence. Although I do not dispute the fact that therapists' talent for attunement can take many forms, and patients can be tuned into via many "channels", as it were, I am suggesting that the direct experience by therapists of their own bodies may strengthen their recognition of the countertransference. This use of the body could be especially helpful in strengthening therapists' ability to differentiate between their own feelings and those that belong to the patient. This will be discussed more fully in Chapters Three and Four.

## Outline of the project

The book is laid out in three major parts. I lay the groundwork in Part I by describing the relevant theory from both disciplines—

psychoanalysis and movement analysis/movement psychotherapy—with the intention of presenting their different points of
view and the different methods, themes, and categories that have
emerged in each. I will describe the disciplines' different ways of
thinking about and perceiving reality, calling attention to elements
within the two languages that support each other or overlap, and to
ways in which they seem to diverge or to define separate domains.

In Part II, I draw upon the theory described in Part I, and inter-
weave the two perspectives in my presentation of data gathered
from four psychoanalytic observational studies. Because the
languages of both movement and psychoanalytic object relations
have their roots in earliest infancy, I have gone directly to the source
by observing infants and young children firsthand.

Refined observation skills are a key element in both movement
psychotherapy and psychoanalysis/psychotherapy. Even where
the primary tool for communication is words, as in any verbal therapy, the body and its movement convey a great deal about what is
beneath or beyond words. I use a blending of movement analysis
and psychoanalytic theory to reflect on the material gathered in the
various observational settings as a way of exploring what can be
gained by consciously interweaving the two perspectives, both in
drawing out themes and reflecting on them.

In Part III, I further explore the potential benefits of this interplay of two languages by applying them to my clinical work with
three adult patients in individual movement therapy. In so doing, I
am exploring how this interweaving of disciplines works in a
"hybrid practice", an approach to movement psychotherapy that is
underpinned by psychoanalytic theory. In particular, I am interested in how such a practice may help bring to light the ways in
which primitive psychophysical patterns, of the kind described in
the infant and young child observations, are represented in adults.

It has been said that Freud explored the child in the adult and
Klein explored the infant in the child. Contemporary Kleinians real-
ize that the infant in the adult also benefits from attention; it is my
hope that this book adds to the resources for making contact with
these primordial traces. A key element in this approach to movement psychotherapy is the somatic aspect of the countertransference as a way of registering the unconscious and primitive
psychodynamics within and between patient and therapist.

## The broad map

Primarily this interdisciplinary study draws together psychoanalytic theory and movement analysis for comparison and synthesis. The ways in which early psychophysical templates are established and held in the body, and the implications of these for psychic and emotional development in later life are the concern of many other disciplines as well. Space does not permit a lengthy description of these in this book, but I wish to make reference to them in order to place my own undertaking in a broader context.

A map of the broader terrain would include the field of infant development research, which has been allied to, and has helped to underpin, psychoanalytic thinking. Melanie Klein's belief that babies are social, object-related beings from the start, for example, is substantiated by infant research. What stands out in filmed sequences by many researchers are the "proto-conversations", the turn-taking, matching of rhythm and expression, which appear to happen even within the first hours of an infant's life. The baby and mother attune to each other through matching internal and external rhythms, and it has been seen that sounds also match the bodily rhythms. In this way they mutually regulate arousal level and positive affect in the baby (Beebe & Lachmann, 1988, 2002; Moscowitz, Monk, Kaye, & Ellman, 1997; Stern, 1985; Tronick, 1987).

Attachment theory, stemming from the work of John Bowlby (1988), takes as a basic premise that infants form patterns of attachment to their key caregivers as a built-in biological survival mechanism. The nature of these non-verbal patterns, based on the opposing themes of attachment and loss/separation, depend on the nature of the relationships during the first year of the infant's life. Through structured research, different discernible patterns of attachment have been observed; classifications of "secure, avoidant, resistant, and disorganized" attachment have evolved (Main & Cassidy, 1988).

A movement-based system used in observing mother–infant interaction and attunement is the Kestenberg Movement Profile (Kestenberg Amighi, Loman, Lewis, & Sossin, 1999). This system is derived from Laban Movement Analysis (LMA) (Bartenieff, 1980; Laban, 1950, 1966), which constitutes a central element in my work. Judith Kestenberg, a psychiatrist and Freudian psychoanalyst, linked her perception of movement to drive theory as defined by Freud (1905d). For my purposes in this work, I found the LMA system to be perfectly adequate for describing movement. I will, therefore, not be elaborating on the extensive work of Kestenberg and her successors.

My work can also be situated within the long established and wide-ranging field of non-verbal communication, which encompasses many practical and philosophical strands. Frances La Barre (2001), herself a psychoanalyst exploring non-verbal behaviour in clinical practice, usefully separates these into three complementary schools.

The first, which she calls the "intrinsic meaning school", has its roots in Darwin's exploration of universal meaning in facial expressions (1872). It considers that there is a common language of the body that is innate and cross-cultural, which we can read by direct intuitive experience.

The "cultural school" emphasized the learned and culturally determined aspects of non-verbal communication. This school has resonance with the psychoanalytic notion of meaning being dependent on context and relationship; it can be said to provide another perspective on that idea by emphasizing the realm of the non-verbal.

The "school of practical analysis" addresses in depth aspects of non-verbal language and their reflection of "human beingness". The key proponent was Rudolf Laban (1950, 1966), elements of whose work will constitute the framework for movement analysis I will be using. These elements, according to La Barre (2001, p. 142), "are especially helpful in developing the psychoanalyst's visual and kinaesthetic senses".

*Evidence from neuroscience*

Recent developments in the field of *neuroscience* have established clear evidence that infants' early experience of emotional and physical contact with their key care-givers stimulates the development of patterns of "wiring and firing" within the brain, which have potentially lifelong effects. This work points to the fact that body, mind, and feelings are inseparable, and, it seems to me, rather significantly paves the way for recognizing patients' and therapists' bodily experience as a valuable tool in any psychotherapy. Allan

Schore (1994) speaks of a process of unconscious transmission of *psychobiological states* from one person to another between their right brains. The right hemisphere of the brain, dominant for body and feeling, is in the ascendant for the first three years of life. Schore explains that the right brain decodes the emotional stimuli by actual felt somatic emotional reactions to the stimuli "in a preverbal bodily based dialogue" (Schore, 2001a, p. 67). This seems to be describing what I would call the language of movement.

It is more helpful, perhaps, to think of the infant's primitive awarenesses as states of "body–mind" than states of mind. To quote Antonio Damasio,

> . . . the body, as represented by the brain, may constitute the indispensable frame of reference for the neural processes that we experience as the mind. . . . [The body] is used as the ground reference for the constructions we make of the world around us and for the construction of the ever-present sense of subjectivity that is part and parcel of our experiences. [Damasio, 1994, p. xvi]

Memory, it follows, is a process which belongs to the "body–mind".

Damasio has described as "Descartes's error" the separation of body and mind at the heart of most Western cultures (Damasio, 1994). Cultural and religious doctrines, which have historically promoted mind–body dualism, have been faced with the new scientific evidence. Aposhyan (1999) traces the cultural splitting between body and mind back to the biblical association of the body with the "fall from grace" and the accompanying legacy of denigrating the body, and imposing strict rules and punishments, linking the body with sin and guilt. In subsequent centuries, in Western cultures' pursuit of pure reason in its investigation of reality, and its strenuous efforts toward controlling nature, the body was pressured to be thought of as an unfeeling object, rather than as a live, feeling entity full of human needs and impulses. Perhaps not until Freud has this reality been confronted and explored.

*Movement as a source of understanding and development*

Another part of the broad terrain includes the experiential nature of movement, the art of acquiring one's own movement vocabulary, towards facilitating non-verbal communication and self under-standing. This practical experience can be gained through many different means. A key resource here, as mentioned, will be Laban Movement Analysis, which, by codifying the range of elements of movement, provides a lexicon of both form and feeling. LMA will be fully explored in Chapter Two, which concentrates on translating the "language of movement" into words.

Amerta Movement, is an *experiential practice* of non-stylized movement which, in my view, both augments LMA and has strong links with psychoanalytic object relations theory. It, too, having a central role in this integration of frameworks, will be described in depth in Chapter Two.

## "Body Mind Centering"

I draw in a more indirect way on "Body Mind Centering" (BMC), a developmental approach to the study of movement evolved by American researcher Bonnie Bainbridge Cohen (1993). BMC has extended a traditional approach to the study of anatomy and physiology by developing an *experiential* analysis of bodily systems—skeletal, muscular, nerves, organs, glands, fluids—each of which has its own characteristic qualities, rhythms, and states of mind. This work seems to concur with the view expressed by many neuroscientists, that the body is indeed "minded" (Damasio, 1994, Panksepp, 1998).

Cohen emphasizes that movement begins in the womb and is itself the first mode of perception. It lays down a baseline for how we process information using other senses. *Embodiment* is defined by Cohen as an integrated relationship between oneself and the world, between the sensations from inside and the perceptions from outside (Cohen, 1993, p. 63). Seen from a psychoanalytic perspective, the relationship between self and object is implied in BMC.

Cohen defines five fundamental actions she feels are basic building blocks in the development of movement. The first is *yielding* to gravity and a primal contact with the object world. The ability to yield and be in touch underlies the ability to take appropriate and effective action. Separating from this contact requires *pushing*. This action gives the ability to sense one's body and mobilize one's own weight, thus empowering one to explore the world. Pushing pro-vides the ground and gives support for *reaching*, which expresses an infant's curiosity, desire, or compassion in extending into space. *Grasping* and *pulling* are the logical extensions of reaching, and are the culmination of successful yielding, pushing, and reaching (Aposhyan, 1999, p. 63).

Cohen's emphasis on the primary quality of "yielding in contact" as the basis for other patterns emerging organically, seems also to resonate with ideas from neuroscience. Whereas neuro-scientists have confirmed that early deprivation or neglect in infancy—which would imply a disturbance in "yielding"—means that important bits of "wiring up" in the brain may be permanently lost, Cohen's work is based on the belief that, even if that is so, it is possible to use movement to restimulate weak neural patterning, discover alternative pathways, and thereby continue to unfold and develop throughout one's lifetime.

## Other related practices

These include Authentic Movement, derived from Carl Jung's "Active Imagination" (1961) and developed as a form of personal development and dance therapy by Mary Whitehouse and, later, Janet Adler (2002) and others. Like Amerta Movement, it shares with psychoanalysis the value of free associative processes in its emphasis on following a spontaneous flow of impulses. As a prac-tice, however, it does not fit with an object relations approach as well as Amerta Movement does. I will refer to Authentic Movement again in Chapter Two.

Body psychotherapy derives from the work on body armour and body energy developed by Wilhelm Reich, an early colleague of Freud. Reich and his successors developed Freud's idea of the body ego; whereas attention to the body tended to fade into the background over time in psychoanalysis, it has always been of central importance in body psychotherapy.

Body psychotherapy often incorporates touch into its work, and in this particular way, it shares some common ground with many forms of bodywork—Alexander Technique, Feldenkrais Method, Rolfing, to name but a few. On the issue of touch, I personally agree with Danielle Quinodoz, (2003, p. 133), who writes ". . . the analys- and would indeed like to be touched physically by the analyst through actions, like a child with incestuous wishes, but, he does not on any account want his wishes to be fulfilled". I am more inter- ested in the development, through psychophysical attunement, of "affective resonance", which can be said to be a form or "non- physical touch" (Charles, 2001).

## In conclusion

This work arises out of my passionate interest over many years in gaining greater understanding of the psychophysical terrain. The bringing of two perspectives together in this book is akin to stand- ing on a bridge between two fields. In my view, the perspective from the bridge provides a kind of "frontier" that can reveal insights into the adjacent territories.

My belief that *integration* can belong neither to the mind nor the body alone, that it involves both, and the two are inseparable, leads me to investigate the following areas of particular interest through- out this book:

- the role movement can play in exploring the interrelationships between psyche and body, with particular emphasis on the primitive defences and unconscious phantasies that stem from infancy and early childhood;
- the relevance of psychoanalytic observational studies of infants and young children in exploring these themes;
- the usefulness of enhanced body awareness, personal experi- ence of movement and a language for movement analysis in any therapist's apprehension of countertransference experi- ence;
- the ongoing development of a psychodynamically informed method of practice in movement psychotherapy.

I hope that this book can stimulate discussion and dialogue about theory and practice within and between movement and psychoanalytic therapies.

## Notes

1. The official title for my profession is more commonly Dance Movement Therapy (DMT). Because I am working with patients' natural movement and without music, I prefer to emphasize "movement" and de-emphasize "dance" and the connotations associated with it; thus, I prefer to use the lesser used title, Movement Psychotherapy. The two names are used more or less interchangeably in the book.

# CHAPTER TWO

# The language of movement: embodying psychic processes

"God guard me from those thoughts men think
In the mind alone;
He that sings a lasting song
Thinks in a marrow-bone"

(From "A Prayer for Old Age" by W. B. Yeats)

I n his BBC television series *The Human Mind* (2003), Professor Robert Winston said, "It seems the key to knowing what people feel is in watching them move." Consciously or unconsciously, our identity is firmly linked to our felt experience of being "bodied". The sensory and emotional experience of the body can be seen to comprise a language of its own that can be attuned to, communicated, and "read". In this chapter, I discuss some ways in which awareness and recognition of bodily experience can be deepened, and the role embodied movement (and stillness) can play in enabling greater access to emotional and psychological processes.

*Overview of this chapter*

I begin by providing two descriptive vignettes that show how deepening one's access to bodily experience can enable a deeper contact with oneself. The first of these is in the field of actor training; the second is from my clinical practice in movement therapy. These vignettes will be a prelude to providing a description of Laban Movement Analysis (LMA), a principally *experiential* language that "translates" human movement in all its manifestations and complexities into words and concepts.

I make use of LMA as a key resource in this book, in the quest to explore the interrelationships between the field of Dance Movement Therapy (DMT) and psychoanalytic theory. LMA is familiar to DMT practitioners as a useful tool in organizing their perceptions of sensoriaffective experience of the body, and in defining patterns used in "coping with the environment" (Bartenieff, 1980). This verbal language for describing movement can help to retrieve sensory experience from what the philosopher Merleau-Ponty describes as "a chaos in which I am submerged" (Merleau-Ponty, 1964), so that it can be received and reflected upon as a major component of self experience.

I follow this by describing Amerta Movement, the work of the Indonesian movement teacher, Suprapto Suryodarmo (known also as Prapto). This body of work, totally experiential and about which little has been written, is based on the non-stylized, natural movement of the body in relationship to both internal and external "landscapes". This work, although derived from very different cultural roots, further illuminates the Labanian concepts, as well as having strong resonances with object relations theory (Bloom, 1994). It is therefore significant in its ability to support the integration of the two theoretical languages I am attempting to bring together. Non-stylized movement, according to Poynor (1998) is "process-oriented . . . It is not prescriptive and is concerned with movement unfolding over time, a journey which is different for each individual, reflecting the uniqueness of their body and personal history". This definition is discussed later with reference to the field of dance movement therapy (DMT).

I give an overview of the field of DMT, and also suggest what I see as the primary goals within the profession, as well as some of the underlying assumptions. I offer some thoughts on the use of LMA as a creative resource in DMT. Finally, I describe my experience using LMA, underpinned by psychoanalytic thinking, in a teaching setting, working with drama students at the Royal Academy of Dramatic Art, where the aim is, in addition to discovering and developing one's own movement vocabulary, to embody psychological and emotional states.

## A glimpse into the language of movement in two practical settings

### In movement training at the Royal Academy of Dramatic Art

Students were asked to devise a physical preparation based on Laban's vocabulary which enabled them to embody their characters' states of mind before presenting a scene. Two students devised the following warm-up for playing the physically and emotionally vulnerable Laura and the confident Jim (the "gentleman caller"), in Tennessee Williams', *Glass Menagerie*. For Laura: the actress started lying down, curling on her side in a foetal position, sensing within herself an anxious internal "wringing" sensation, while imagining that all around her she perceived unidentifiable sounds, which cause her attention to "flick" from one place to another. She then stood and walked in the space. Though she no longer thought about these images, she was still affected by the preparation.

As Jim, the actor also chose to begin close to the floor by pressing his hands very deliberately against it, then pressing other body parts just as deliberately—his head, pelvis, ribs with the intention of "gaining strength in every part of my body". He did this with his eyes closed. When he opened his eyes he told himself "I own all that I can see", and that he was "loved even by the air I breathe". After sensing each other in the space, the two actors were ready to engage in the scene.

### In clinical movement therapy practice

A young woman relatively new to movement therapy came to a session approaching a holiday break feeling very agitated. She felt she wanted to "develop movement vocabulary" for expressing these feelings. As I received the impact of her intense bodily energy, I asked if she felt like standing up as a way of spreading the feelings through her body. She did. I stood too, with her agreement. Still sensing her accumulated emotional energy, I asked if she wanted to walk around a little with her feelings. She said yes, but took one step and realized she felt she could not go on. Her energy was totally bound in a frozen position. I inquired into her experience, asking what the inability to move was like. She described her frustration intensifying, and said she felt the urge to "tear someone apart".

Speaking about what she felt, she began to reach forward and twist her fists as if wringing the guts from someone; she stomped with rage and slashed the air as she continued to describe her destructive fantasies. She then sat and tearfully expressed her shock and shame at what had emerged. As she and I digested the effects of these dark feelings, which had not previously appeared in our work, she saw that I could help her to think about how the primitive feelings were partly stirred by feeling abandoned by me in the approaching break; she experienced a sense of relief that I could stand up to and meet this part of her, and that it could be safely included in the work.

## *Verbalizing the non-verbal*

Movement, taken in a broad sense, is always the basis for change (Resnik, 1995). Attending to physical sensation and movement can support recognition of psychic states, and provide a way of relating to them so that they may become more flexible and transparent. It can be said that the body exists in the here and now. Although it is shaped by both the hopes and wishes for the future and the experiences and memories of the past, it exists concretely in the present. But the body is more than a concrete reality; it also reflects unconscious introjective and projective processes. Of special significance are those of earliest infancy. (This will be elaborated in Chapter Three.) Psychoanalyst Danielle Quinodoz suggests that "when a patient has been deeply affected by early experiences, it is the re-experiencing of the bodily experience that will enable him to recover his unrecognised affects and his bodily fantasies" (Quinodoz, 2003, p. 104). This premise is central to the use of movement in healing and therapy. The preverbal language of infancy can be said to be at the root of non-verbal communication through movement.

In experiencing the body more deeply we build bridges between different modes of experience—cognitive, sensory, and affective. By balancing these different modes, one aspect of self experience is not so easily used as a defence against another. Links can be made between body, mind, and feelings that help support awareness of what parts of the self have been abandoned, what patterns have become entrenched. In my view, the language of movement can provide one way to describe and articulate the subtle but significant comings and goings, openings and closings that define the therapeutic process.

Throughout this chapter I hope to provide more than a descriptive discussion of the various themes; rather, it is my hope and intention to convey an experiential feel for the language of movement. Because the medium here is words, and the medium of movement is by definition non-verbal, this will perhaps require that readers meet me half-way, so to speak, by allowing themselves to absorb and embody the language, to take it inside, and feel the effects of the different experiences described.

As a preparation for more easily absorbing the following section—a lengthy (and potentially otherwise dry) description of a language which provides words for identifying a wide range of psychological and emotional states in movement terms—perhaps it is advisable that readers take a moment now to become a little more aware of their physical experience:

> *Pause to take a breath and slow the mind down, to feel the position of your body; to feel the whole shape the body inhabits, to experience the effect of gravity and the contact with the chair, to feel parts of the body in this position, perhaps with closed eyes but not necessarily—the belly . . . the chest . . . the legs . . . the back . . . the face . . . to allow a little time to be receptive to the sensations, the feelings that arise, the perception of the surrounding space from this position . . . In this way, the reader can perhaps feel a rebalancing of attention, what could be said to be a more three-dimensional embodying of the mind and feelings. Perhaps readers will experience a wish to move a little, to change their position in some way, to give the body more space . . .*

I have suggested this experiential interlude in the hope that the reader can give time to absorb the following material not only cognitively, but experientially.

*Laban Movement Analysis*

"The integrating power of movement is its most important value for the individual" (Laban, 1966, p. 112).

Rudolf Laban (1879–1958) was a pioneer in the field of movement observation, analysis, and research. His perceptions led to the formation of a detailed vocabulary for describing human movement. Laban Movement Analysis (LMA) allows for great subtlety and specificity in distinguishing between a wide range of different components, both quantitative and qualitative. It is increasingly recognized world-wide in the fields of dance movement therapy and in the performing arts as a common language for communication about movement. Laban also developed a system for movement notation that, even in the age of video recording, is still widely used as a way to capture the live three-dimensional experience. Although Laban did not promote a specific method for change, his focus throughout his life was on the *process* of movement, as a means of expression and communication, a means of developing the kinaesthetic sense and awakening creativity.

Laban was born in what is now Bratislava in the Czech Republic. He emigrated to England during the 1940s, where he and his followers developed and applied his movement research within the areas of education, in work settings, in therapy and rehabilitation, as well as his initial base in dance and theatre. "He left to generations of movement professionals an oeuvre with seemingly unlimited possibilities for interpretation and implementation" (Maletic, 1987, p. 27).

Laban developed a comprehensive vocabulary within two major branches of theory to define the basic principles of movement. I will concentrate on Eukinetics, later called Effort theory, which describes the inner impulses that lead one into movement. The other, Space Harmony, is a detailed analysis of the relationship between the body and the surrounding space. All movement can be described in terms of Effort, Space Harmony, and body/shape. Laban (1950, p. 2) wrote that

> Movement is the result of the striving after an object deemed valuable, or of a state of mind. Its shapes and rhythms show the moving person's attitude in a particular situation. It can characterize

momentary mood and reaction as well as constant features of personality.

## Effort theory

Eukinetics, translated into English as *Effort theory*, is concerned with the expressive, qualitative aspect of movement and will, therefore, be of utmost importance in thinking about the relationship between movement and psychic and emotional states. It pertains to *how* a movement is performed and is thus more related to feeling than form. In what manner does a person perform a task or gesture? What is the quality of expression conveyed by the movement (or stillness)? How could one define the specific quality of "effort" involved?

## Basic Effort elements

Laban identified four Effort elements (Table 1) that seemed to be motivating factors in one's choice of how to move, even before any visible movement is made. Laban defined the four properties that spark or motivate movement (in response to internal or external, conscious or unconscious impulses) as *weight, space, time,* and *flow*. He also named two qualities to define either end of a spectrum of possibilities in describing how each quality could be manifested, elaborated as follows.

The element of *weight*, designated as *strong* or *light*, relates to the physical *sensation* of the body itself, the skin, the muscles, the literal,

*Table 1.*   Basic Effort elements.

| Quality | Association | Realm of experience stimulated |
|---|---|---|
| Weight (strong or light) | Intention | Physical sensation/Impact |
| Space (direct or flexible) | Attention | Thought/Orientation/Perspective |
| Time (sudden or sustained) | Decision | Intuition/Pace |
| Flow (bound or free) | Progression | Feelings/Control |

material substance, both surface and depth of the body, and the sense of touch. In bringing this aspect of experience to life, through making it conscious, Laban suggested that one develops an *intention* to work with, to do something with the body. Usually this something is done in relation to others, who are either available or not to one's intentions towards them. The element of weight, then, is related to one's sense of agency, one's ability to have an impact, as well as to be an "in-formed" being. A sense of three-dimensional presence provides a place from which to feel, see, or think. For this reason, I consider this element to be of central importance.

> *Perhaps the reader would like to activate the body weight, by strong stretching, and/or attention to the more delicate sensation of lightness in sensing the skin, and the clothing against the skin.*

The element of *space* relates to one's *attention* to the outside world, one's perspective, one's particular point of view; it engages the *mental* aspect of personality in a sharp, *direct* focus or a *flexible*, broad overview. (It must be clarified that this use of the word space differs from that implied by Space Harmony. Whereas the latter is used to describe the form of movement, the space effort refers to the quality of focus or attention to the outside world.) Just as weight is concerned with the realm of physical experience, space is concerned with the realm of the mind. The challenge, it can be said, is to embody the mind, rather than thinking and imagining from a place split off from the body and feelings, so that one can feel oneself to be inside one's narrative, so to speak, and not objectively describing it from a distance.

> *Perhaps the reader would like to feel the effect of taking in the outside world through the eyes, receiving the view . . . observing the different quality of mental awareness when taking in the details and when absorbing the more spacious, flexible overview.*

The element of *time* is related to the *impulses, decisions, rhythms, and phrasing*. The experience of time within oneself, in the outside world, and intersubjectively, the realization of the natural order of events and change is an inherent and intuitive aspect of human experience. The experience of choices and transitions is linked with the element of time. Suryodarmo puts the challenge to be IN time rather than only ON time, an idea that reflects his Buddhist background. In Laban's vocabulary, time has a quality of *accelerating—*

*"sudden" movement or decelerating*—*"sustained" movement,* of urgency or leisureliness.

> *Perhaps the reader can attend to the counterpointed internal rhythms of heartbeat and breathing as references to time which can form a backdrop to allowing a little movement to happen in the body or parts thereof—as if "listening" to the rhythm, phrasing or "music" of the movement.*

Finally, the element of *flow* is associated with the *continuity* of movement, how *bound or free* a movement is, the relative freedom or restriction of the flow of breath and energy or "life force". This element has a bearing on the control or release of feelings, the experience of emotion in the body. Of interest is how the flow of energy and feelings opens toward or closes away from relationship. Flow also speaks more practically of the degree of control or *precision* in movement.

> *Perhaps readers can close their eyes in order to experience either the places where energy is bound and muscles are tightening to hold feelings back, or the melting of such tension and the subtle release of feeling which may wish to sequence through the body in free movement. There may be fluctuation between binding and freeing of flow.*

## States and drives

Effort theory goes on to define *states* and *drives*. These are the result of Laban's analysis of the complexity of behaviour as defined by Effort qualities. He observed that two of the four basic elements are usually motivating a person at any time, while the other two, though present, remain in the background. For example, a lazy stretch upon waking up would likely involve a combination of weight and flow, the physical and emotional elements; whereas an intense response to paintings as one strolls through an exhibition might tend to involve space and flow, denoting the mental and emotional realms. These combinations of two qualities each have a name that broadly describes a state of mind. In the preceding examples, the former is *dream state*, the latter *remote state*. The others are as follows.

Time and weight creates a mood called *near state*, a felt sense of embodied rhythm—a person who is on a mission, who knows "where they are coming from", to use a common phrase. The physical and the intuitive aspects are activated.

Time and space is called *awake state*, an outwardly focused state of alertness and decision—the mental and intuitive aspects are activated. A spectator at a tennis match may characterize this alert state.

Space and weight denote *stable state*, combining the physical and mental aspects; this combination gives a strong sense of active presence and mental perspective, someone thoughtfully standing his ground, undeterred.

Time and flow combines feelings and impulses, the *mobile state*, an impulsive and changeable, often playful mood.

There are three pairs of opposite states; and within each state, there are four possible combinations of the two effort qualities, giving a range of possible ways of experiencing each state. For example, within dream state, the possibilities are: strong (weight) and free (flow), strong and bound, light and free, and light and bound. Each of the four, as one hopes the reader can sense within themselves, is quite distinct from the others. The six states of mind are as shown below.

*States of mind*

| Dream | = | Weight | + | Flow |
|---|---|---|---|---|
| Awake | = | Time | + | Space |
| Near | = | Weight | + | Time |
| Remote | = | Space | + | Flow |
| Mobile | = | Time | + | Flow |
| Stable | = | Weight | + | Space |

In trying to get a feel for the different states of mind, it is useful to consider not only which elements are motivating someone, but also which are absent. It is hoped that the reader can recognize the effects of attuning to the various pairs of elements, or realms of experience.

*Action drive*

Drives, as opposed to states, combine *three* active Effort elements at once. The *Action Drive*, in which the emotional element of flow is in the background, can be described in terms of its particular combinations of the movement qualities of weight, space,

and time. Moving a piano, for example involves *pressing*—strong/
sustained/direct; but pressing can describe a person's mental and
emotional attitude as well (North, 1972). The eight *Effort actions*
that make up the action drive were given the names displayed
below.

*Effort actions*

| Action | | Weight | | Space | | Time |
|--------|---|--------|---|--------|---|-----------|
| Float | = | Light | + | Flexible | + | Sustained |
| Punch | = | Strong | + | Direct | + | Sudden |
| Glide | = | Light | + | Direct | + | Sustained |
| Slash | = | Strong | + | Flexible | + | Sudden |
| Wring | = | Strong | + | Flexible | + | Sustained |
| Dab | = | Light | + | Direct | + | Sudden |
| Flick | = | Light | + | Flexible | + | Sudden |
| Press | = | Strong | + | Direct | + | Sustained |

*Transformation drives*

Like the Effort actions, *transformation drives* (Table 2) are motivated
by *three* of the basic elements at once (unlike the states of mind
which are motivated by two elements). When flow is an active
element it is said to replace one of the other three, thus transforming the action into a highly emotional drive. The spaceless *Passion
Drive*, in which weight, time, and flow are active, is characterized
by uncensored emotional and physical expression—the ability to
reflect, associated with space, is absent. In the timeless *Spell Drive*,
space, weight, and flow are active; this drive can be used to control
others or in extreme fear, for example. In the weightless *Vision
Drive*, space, time, and flow are active; this can create a disembodied emotional and imaginative excitement. When someone is

*Table 2.*   Transformation drives.

| Drive | Defining characteristic |
|-------|-------------------------|
| Spell | Timeless (weight–space–flow) |
| Vision | Weightless (Time–space–flow) |
| Passion | Spaceless (weight–time–flow) |

very intensely emotionally involved in an experience, do they (1) lose all awareness of time—*spell drive*? (2) lose all awareness of weight—*vision drive*? or (3) lose all awareness of space—*passion drive*?

Although it is hard to convey the various experiences of Laban's Effort theory without guiding the reader in experiential work, I hope to have stimulated readers' interest in the potential for links being made between the four basic elements composing movement dynamics—and the innumerable combinations and patterns in which they appear—and the psychodynamics of internal and inter-personal relationships that is the focus of Chapter Three.

## Space Harmony

"In order to study harmony of movement we must consider the relations between the architecture of the human body and the spatial structure of the kinesphere" (Laban, 1966).

This aspect of Laban's work concerns the body's relationship to, and orientation in, the surrounding space. As psychoanalytic object relations theory emphasizes the context in which events happen, and the primacy of relationship, this part of Laban's theory also has resonance with psychotherapy and psychoanalysis; this is expanded in Chapter Four. Laban wrote that "space is a hidden feature of movement and movement is a visible aspect of space" (Laban, 1966, p. 4). He saw movement as describing "trace forms" in space. He defined the space around one's body as one's personal reach space or "kinesphere", and he described the dimensions, planes, and diagonals within this personal space as they related to the centre of gravity of the body. By connecting their various points, he visualized geometric forms surrounding the body. The icosa-hedron results from the connecting of peripheral points of the three planes—vertical, horizontal, and sagittal—when they are super-imposed.

This form was seen to be the most naturally related to human movement. Laban described the dynamic interrelationship between the body and points in space as "spatial tensions" and "counter-tensions" between two or more directions at once. These so-called tensions were the "springboards for mobility" (see Figure 1).

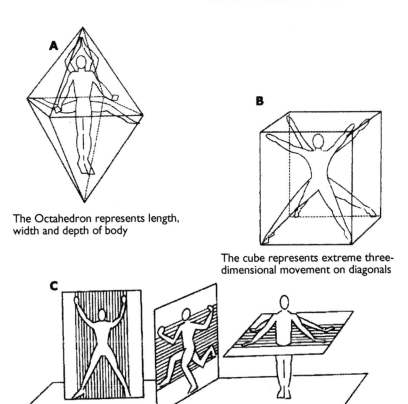

The Octahedron represents length, width and depth of body

The cube represents extreme three-dimensional movement on diagonals

Two-dimensional planes—nicknamed door, wheel and table respectively

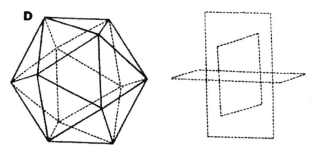

Icosahedron, developed from overlap of three planes, represents modified diagonals

*Figure 1.*   Spatial orientation related to the three dimensions: height, width and depth. (Source: Maletic, 1987)

*LMA in Dance Movement Therapy*

At its best, LMA offers a set of tools for dance movement therapists to more precisely and accurately recognize and describe patients' movement patterns and preferences. At the same time, LMA offers a framework that can support therapists' ability to embody their own experience, thus enabling them to more genuinely empathize with patients. It must be said, however, that the use of LMA to facilitate the understanding of patients' communication may also invite a prescribed, potentially overly objectifying and diagnostic way of working with patients. Laban supplied categories that, like any theory, including psychoanalytic theory, can be employed within a clinical setting as a way of avoiding the emotional impact of what is happening.

DMT is explicitly involved with the examination of the interrelationships between non-verbal communication and psychic and emotional states. A question that underlies this chapter is whether aspects of DMT and the language of movement, by bringing physical sensation and bodily expression into the foreground, may have anything to offer to psychotherapy, psychoanalytic observational study and psychoanalysis in addressing the non-verbal or preverbal levels in which many patients' more primitive defences are based.

*The pioneers*

Dance Movement Therapy grew out of the work of a handful of "pioneers" in the USA in the 1950s, women who were working independently of each other, on opposite sides of the country. In describing this period, one of these pioneers, Irmgard Bartenieff, who founded the Laban Institute of Movement Studies in New York in 1978, writes that almost all of these women stumbled into their work "by accident" from their earlier careers teaching and/or performing dance. They began to offer group sessions, usually in psychiatric settings, based on their common belief that "it is possible to reach people's feelings through the exciting, enlivening and calming power of dance" (Bartenieff, 1980, p. 143).

Bartenieff brought Laban's work to the USA from Germany in the 1940s. She was subsequently invited to employ the Laban vocabulary in working with psychiatric patients in a New York City hospital. The appeal of Laban's work to Dr Israel Zwerling, the psychiatrist who supported this innovative venture, was that movement could be described objectively and precisely, using its own terms, thus avoiding the depersonalized labelling and classifying of patients into standard psychiatric categories. Through movement analysis, patients could be more subtly thought about as distinct individuals.

*The Chacian approach*

Perhaps the key figure in the development of DMT was Marion Chace, who brought her work in improvisational dance to a federal psychiatric hospital in Washington, DC, where she worked with the most disturbed and non-verbal patients. The model developed by Chace, which emphasizes group unity and interaction, remains the primary model used in DMT. The ritualistic, unifying experience of dancing together in a circle was felt to provide a safe container for these patients. The circle was felt to be "an organic expression of non-aggressive relationship" that "aids the experience of streams of movement energy spreading from one to the other" (Bartenieff, 1980, p. 1).

Groups were typically led in a warm-up, the purpose of which was to "mobilize the group's capacity for emotional expression and social interaction" (Lewis, 1979, p. 27). A follow-the-leader structure was often used, which, depending on the degree of emotional disturbance, might provide individuals in the group with the chance to take the lead. Rhythm was used as a tool for creating a sense of solidarity and a contagious enlivening of the emotional atmosphere. The shared experience of vitality and mobility seem to have been key goals.

Chace did not work from a theoretical model and had no particular background in or experience of psychotherapy. Yet she obviously had some implicit assumptions and intuitive principles that guided her. She recognized that her work allowed patients who were unable to find the means of communicating with others to find support for expressing feelings within the context of the group. She described a patient thus: "As his feeling of isolation and his fear of a lack of understanding are reduced, he is able to put aside autistic expression to an increasing degree" (Chodorow, 1991, p. 30). She also knew intuitively that music could be used as a catalyst in engaging with patients—to enliven them, and to reflect, develop, or alter a particular mood. Chace did articulate many goals in relation to the work that pointed towards a deep interest in the integration of body and mind, and of verbal and non-verbal expression. But it is said that "she never treated anyone, she just danced with them" (Dyrud, 1993).

In emphasizing the group experience and group cohesiveness, the Chacian approach necessarily de-emphasizes patients' unique, individual experience and expression. Chace obviously felt that striving for individual expression and integrity was not as important or as possible in the settings in which she worked as the power of the group to stimulate the individual and to reflect the individual back to herself. The group itself is the medium for change, and individuals in a group can potentially experience themselves via projection into others within the group. "The more group members can see and feel their every experience to be meaningful to the group as a whole, (the more) their basic matrix of self is remobilized and worked through in the new group field" (Pines, 1984).

*Active imagination—a Jungian approach*

Other pioneers, as well as successive generations of DMTs, have linked their work to a variety of psychological frameworks. Mary Whitehouse, who worked in Los Angeles around the same time as Chace worked in Washington, combined her background as a dancer with her interest as a student of, and patient in, Jungian analysis in the development of her approach to DMT. She brought Jung's notion of "active imagination" (1961) to bear on her work. Active imagination described the intention to bring the unconscious into play, usually through the channel of an art-form such as drawing or writing. Whitehouse felt this state could also be stimulated through movement. She differentiated between "the experience of letting it happen, in contrast to doing it". Whitehouse said, "Movement, to be experienced, has to be *found* in the body, not put on like a dress or a coat" (Chodorow, 1991, p. 27).

It would seem that Whitehouse was exploring what could be thought of as a free associative process in movement. This attitude

led her away from using the term "dance". "I had to call it movement. I needed to give up images in them and in myself of what
it meant to dance" (Lewis, 1979, p. 63). In this respect, I am aligned
with Whitehouse. Whitehouse's recognition that movement was a
vehicle for embodying and communicating unconscious processes
was an important achievement. She explored this premise in her
work with groups of students and with individual patients. Her
work was less focused on the group and more on the individual,
promoting a focus on internal experience as the basis for a spontaneous and authentic translation of impulse into movement. By
implication, this approach would seem to reach a patient on a
different level.

*Authentic Movement*

This application of active imagination to movement has evolved
into a practice known today as Authentic Movement. Using this
approach, a mover closes her eyes and waits for an "authentic"
impulse, which she then follows into moving. She is watched by a
witness/therapist who, after the allotted time for moving (usually
around twenty minutes) may give feedback about her own experience as observer, if the mover wishes. A question I have about this
way of working concerns its emphasis on waiting for the authentic
impulse to stimulate movement, and whether, like a striving
toward authentic free association, one can run the risk of stifling
spontaneity. There is an implication that what is not "authentic" is
not useful in communicating the patient's condition and phantasies. Does it imply, therefore, an undervaluing of the recognition
and interpretation of resistance and defence?

    Authentic Movement also seems to make certain assumptions
about how to achieve authenticity, for example, the emphasis on
moving exclusively with eyes closed. This is presumably meant to
bring the mover more easily in touch with unconscious material,
but if overemphasized leads to a practice in which authenticity is
linked to making oneself "blind".

    An overemphasis on internal sensing can be a way of escaping
the vicissitudes of relationship and separation. Speaking about
"internal sensing", Bonnie Bainbridge Cohen said,

If it's carried too far there's self-absorption; there's a certain awareness that this is me, but not an awareness that you're you. If it's just
about what's me and not what's not me, then there's no counter-
balance, no definition. [Cohen, 1993, p. 65]

This echoes the central principle of psychoanalytic object relations,
as I detail in Chapter Three. Cohen emphasizes that "A lot of sensing work is an escape from the emotions; it actually represses
emotional integration if it's not balanced" (*ibid.*).

When Authentic Movement is used as a form of therapy (rather
than among a group of colleagues), then the assumption that no
verbal enquiry should be made by the therapist until after the
movement is finished would probably hamper freely developing
transference and countertransference processes. It seems to me that
both the Chacian model and the Authentic Movement model in the
field of DMT, though having clear relevance to working in specific
settings, tend to represent rather extreme positions—the former
risks being overly outwardly focused; the latter risks being overly
internally focused. It seems to me that Amerta Movement suggests
a model that is more equally intra- and inter-personally based.

### Examining goals and implicit assumptions
### in the practice of DMT

Although various approaches to DMT have been developed since
the early days, with a variety of theoretical underpinnings, some
basic principles and methods of practice seem to have remained
constant. A key goal now, as then, is seen to be "the improvement
of patients' ability to form and maintain interpersonal relationships
and the facilitation of their functioning as members of a group"
(Stanton, 1992, p. 124).

The best way to facilitate this goal of eliciting togetherness and
trust in a group is seen to be the employment of exercises and other
structures that will unify the group members. These elements are
especially evident at the beginning of the session, when there is
usually a physical warm-up directed by the therapist. The *circle
formation* is seen to provide a tightly held container, and this
support is enhanced by moving in unison. It is common for patients

to say how they are feeling before the warm-up begins, but the emphasis is on shifting the mood in order to improve the patients' conditions. The leader/therapist will often take a cue from one person's gesture or rhythm to set the group going in a mirroring or follow-the-leader style warm-up.

The use of music to support the creation of group rhythms is also common practice. The automatic use of music to create a particular atmosphere will also contribute to the pattern of lifting patients out of their current emotional state and supplanting it with another. Undoubtedly, this can be a very helpful way of effecting change, particularly in chronically dissociated or depersonalized patients; but in other cases, might the emphasis on changing the status quo be perceived by patients as an artificial or arbitrary pressure for change? It may be premature for some in a group, even if it stimulates a much appreciated change for others.

For some groups, which can be said to be operating on developmentally primitive levels, this kind of warm-up, with its intention to unify and "marshal" a group, seems completely appropriate. The overpowering goal in certain settings for gaining group focus and allaying anxiety could not be managed in any other way. But such a *modus operandi* is implicitly at odds with the therapist taking a neutral stance, one in which she is not seen to be directive or giving advice.

There is more interest nowadays in exploring themes that do not necessarily encourage people to all move in the same way, thereby ameliorating the degree of leadership taken by the therapist and giving patients more space to discover meaningful movement vocabulary of their own, to be seen to do so by others who also do the same. This affords patients the opportunity to be more fully recognized as themselves, rather than only as mirror images of each other. Therapists are well aware that mirroring may at times induce a limited kind of mimicking which can result in a two-dimensional, adhesive type relating.

After the warm-up in Chacian DMT, a session usually proceeds with the development of themes that may arise from the gestures, movement patterns, or feelings that are generated from the warm-up. A theme is usually identified and named. Props, like balls or pieces of fabric, are typically used to help develop the theme and support the focus of attention and energy. The goal is to move from the purely expressive movement of the warm-up to the recognition of symbol formation.

As psychoanalyst Hanna Segal points out, the ability to symbolize is important not only for the patient's ability to communicate with the therapist, but also the ability to communicate with himself. The capacity to find symbols is the basis for verbal thinking (Segal, 1986, p. 58). Again, I wonder whether, in some cases, the preference for guiding the group to find a single theme that can be designated to name the experience of all participants, may limit the exploration of individual differences of association to particular movements. The session is gradually brought to a finish, usually with time for verbal reflection to help integrate the experience.

Clearly, the way a therapist works is partly determined by the needs and limitations of a group. A therapist working with children with extremely challenging behaviour felt that a very structured group with firm boundaries gave patients a sense of being contained, so that they could better contain themselves. Equally, a therapist working with Alzheimer patients used the tight circle and the structured warm-up as a way of stimulating the body memory. It was felt that this gave patients the means for awakening a sense of vitality. "They cannot connect through the mind. At first, they don't know someone is beside them. Their sense of space comes from the movement" (M. Violets, 2000, personal communication). She encouraged patients to venture into the middle to take a solo turn while still feeling held within the circle.

Other therapists I interviewed for this book, who worked with group populations that included anorexic and self harming young women, male refugees, mental health outpatients, psychiatric adult inpatients, women recovering from drug and alcohol abuse, and autistic adults at a day centre, felt they could not zoom in for very long in order to give attention to single individuals within the group. A group focus seemed to be encouraged throughout.

An underlying assumption occasionally associated with DMT is the suggestion that, through a cathartic experience in a movement session, a patient can regain a fundamental sense of wholeness, and that through this experience something can be irrevocably changed. This idea of a sudden transformation, which may or may not have any verbal insight connected with it, is probably misleading in terms of the way therapy of any kind actually works, and the time it takes to effect lasting change.

Perhaps related to this issue is whether to describe the work as "dance" or "movement", or to use the possibly confusing hybrid "dance movement". To my mind, "dance" is more susceptible to suggesting a cathartic healing, whereas "movement" suggests a more gradual working through; but this may be purely personal. Perhaps more thought could be given to the appropriate word to describe the work in various settings; I would argue that, contrary to what is sometimes said in DMT, the two words are not interchangeable.

DMT is still a relatively young profession whose recognition is growing. Pioneering and adventurous work is flourishing throughout the world. I am particularly interested in the development of DMT as it is practised with individual patients; and I am interested in exploring how psychoanalytic thinking can support and deepen the understanding of unconscious psychological and emotional processes in DMT, as practised with both individuals and groups.

## Amerta Movement—an object relations approach

The work of Suprapto Suryodarmo, an Indonesian movement teacher whose non-stylized movement practice derives from his relationship with the natural world, offers valuable insights into the integrative power of movement as a medium for psychophysical integration. When I worked with Prapto in Indonesia, where he lives, and various places in Europe where he taught, I was struck by the similarities between his study of human experience through movement, and ideas drawn from psychoanalytic thinking of which he knew nothing (Bloom, 1994). Yet, because both points of view derive from experience and observation, it is perhaps not so surprising that the principles arising from them are much the same.

"Prapto uses his own body movement as a diagnostic tool, a barometer, to sense what is evolving or trying to emerge in a person's life, or in the interaction between people of different cultures" (Kemp-Welch, 2001). It could be said that Prapto works with what in therapy would be understood as the transference and countertransference. It is my feeling that this approach has much to offer in thinking about practice in DMT.

Suryodarmo refers to Amerta Movement as engendering "response-ability"—the ability to respond to self, other, and the atmosphere and surroundings. His work stimulates awareness of the body's structure and its three-dimensional form, contained by the skin. Students of Amerta are encouraged to be in the here and now, finding the time and space that embodies not only the present, but is also acknowledged to incorporate and reflect the movers' personal and cultural backgrounds. Students develop the movement vocabulary that embodies their own sensory, perceptual, and emotional experience from moment to moment. For Suryodarmo, movement provides a "bridge to understanding" and growth. This process has much in common with free association, which is discussed in the next chapter.

Suryodarmo speaks of discovering a sense of proportion through movement—not too big or too small, too fast or too slow, to feel safe, comfortable, and present. His own cultural background is based in a close relationship to the natural world, and therefore the source of his approach is the human *organism*. He perceives the more Western approach to be based in what he calls *organization*, derived from thoughts, hopes, and dreams, the source of which is human nature.

Verbal therapy, for Suryodarmo, belongs to what he calls the "dream world" which is linked to "organization". This is distinguished from the "reality world" of physical, material existence, linked to the source of "organism". These distinctions could at first glance be seen as a facile division of East and West, but one aim of the movement practice is to recognize these as two aspects of the self, which can be integrated through movement. One could describe it as the embodiment of thoughts and feelings, hopes and dreams. (This notion is brought into relationship with ideas of Wilfred Bion, among others, in Chapter Three.)

Prapto does not refer to his work as therapy; but he has referred to himself as a "gardener". He describes the garden as being the space in between the protected world of home and the outside world of society. This could also be thought of as a description of the Winnicottian "transitional space", between the merger with mother and the separation from her. The area in between is a space where there is potential for creativity and meaningful play to take place.

As Suryodarmo moves with students, he supports them in dealing with whatever is arising, in their efforts to give form to and become "in-formed" by what they are doing—through embodying, expressing, or containing their feelings, wishes, and needs. With Suryodarmo, this is usually a non-verbal process that he has described, when things are flowing, as a process of "irrigation".

In working with groups in Amerta Movement, one aim is to develop "a common field of understanding", in which clear communication can be achieved. This is different from, as Suryodarmo describes it, unconsciously being absorbed by or absorbing others, which limits one's ability to express oneself clearly. In Suryodarmo's view, if all participants "stick to each other" in moving in unison, they are not really communicating. I feel this work can support DMTs in dealing with the complexities of group interaction.

In my opinion, Amerta Movement could have a place in advancing the training of psychotherapists as well as DMTs, as it offers a skill that is often overlooked—how to make one's own three-dimensional bodily experience more conscious as a container for receiving the transference, projective identification, and countertransference more fully. This work could support a clearer recognition of what happens when therapists become enmeshed, overwhelmed, or unconsciously absorbed by interactions with patients.

*Verbal language arising from movement*

Suryodarmo not only offers principles and themes for personal and interpersonal movement practice, but he also finds a way of using (the English) language that comes directly from his background. His way of discovering verbal language from the embodied language of movement from the perspective of "organism", as he calls it, may have relevance in thinking about the relationship between verbal and non-verbal processes in a therapeutic context. When he speaks of being "in-formed", for example, he is referring to an organic, bodily-based experience. Might a different way of recognizing and articulating experience in psychotherapy emerge from a more conscious embodiment of emotional states; and if so, could this have relevance for accessing and working with more primitive material? Psychoanalyst Danielle Quinodoz, in her search for "words that touch", considers a similar idea; she suggests that some patients "need the analyst's discourse to awaken or reawaken bodily phantasies in them so as to be able to find emotional meaning in forgotten sensory experiences . . . [which] will then become a point of departure for mental representation" (Quinodoz, 2003).

I have begun, in this chapter, to make links between movement therapy and psychoanalytic concepts. I develop this further in the next chapter, in which the mental representation of bodily experience is the focus. The overarching question of the interrelationships between the body's movement and psychic and emotional states is addressed further by thinking about whether and how the movement work outlined in this chapter has anything to offer towards the "embodiment" and "digesting" of the aspects of psychoanalytic theory that are put forward in Chapter Three. Can the language of movement inform the psychoanalytic language and vice versa?

### The application of LMA as a resource in the training of actors

There was a startling change in the quality of experience itself when imagination was brought down to earth and made incarnate in the body, a sudden richness that was like the sun coming out over a world that had been all greyness. And not only did the weather change in one's soul when imagination was made incarnate and took its flesh upon it, but the very way one moved was affected. [Milner, 1950, p. 112]

I would like to describe my experience of what the LMA framework and the exploration of its interrelationships with psychoanalytic thinking, underpinned by my study and practice of Suryodarmo's approach to non-stylized movement practice, have collectively brought to the teaching of movement in an educational setting, with particular reference to my work at the Royal Academy of Dramatic Art. I have developed a method of teaching Laban based movement at RADA since 1989. One implicit goal of this work is to explore the links between embodied movement and psychological and emotional states in the actor's process of transformation. The classes provide the space to discover, through the use of movement, the interrelationships between one's inner world and the external or interpersonal world, from the perspective of both the actor and the character—this applies to a sense of "character" that may spontaneously arise from exploring movement, as well as characters from plays that are deliberately explored in the movement lessons. Either way, this method promotes an integrated experience for the actor of being inside the skin rather than "playing" a character but being somewhat separate from the experience.

Using LMA, I provide starting points for organic explorations in movement, usually based on the Effort theory and the elements of weight, space, time, and flow. These starting points give actors the freedom to explore the depth and complexity of characters' experience, and to contact the feelings that underlie, precede, and prompt a line of thought, a choice of words, a need to give form to expression. In a non-stylized movement practice influenced by Amerta Movement, students learn to embody their true experience from moment to moment, to intuitively respond to both inner and outer sources of motivation. Such exploration gives rise to physical characteristics of character—via body attitude, gestures, tone of voice, ways of moving through space, facial expressions, activities, etc., elements of the subtext are conveyed. With the aid of LMA they develop their own movement vocabulary as well as patterns of thought and speech. LMA encourages them to explore a range of possible choices and thereby build their own depth of embodied understanding, drawn from recognizing and responding to their own felt experience.

The eminent teacher Stanislavski called for a "psycho technique" in his later years, which was to be based on the discovery of a logical line of "physical actions". He spoke of the search for "a truly organic embodiment" of the character (Toporkov, 1979). Another renowned teacher, Michael Chekhov wrote:

Psychophysical exercises must be found and applied. First and foremost is extreme sensitivity of the body to the psychological creative impulses. This cannot be achieved by strictly physical exercises. The psychology itself must take part in such development. [Chekhov, 2002]

It seems to me that the integration of LMA with psychoanalytic thinking, underpinned by the work of Suryodarmo, provides precisely what these teachers suggested was necessary for training. As in a therapy setting, a safe and boundaried space is created in which students can enter the unknown and, one hopes, take risks. Part of the challenge for students is to tolerate not knowing exactly what will emerge. The value of free association is instilled as an implicit goal in the work. Safety is provided in part by the LMA framework; but also, by learning to trust the logic of what is unfolding in the moment, students learn to desist from prematurely making conscious decisions and foreclosing deep exploratory work. My own familiarity with the anxiety that can arise in existing in "the unknown" supports me in holding the anxiety for the group. It is a poignant experience to see students slowly recognize and drop their defensive positions and allow themselves to be seen. Ute Hagen describes the actors' intention

> to make myself, for ultimate expression, more vulnerable than in life. I want to remove the mask I might normally use as a cover. What you reveal and do when you are truly vulnerable and wounded is totally different from when, as in life, your purpose is, so often, to prove that you are invulnerable. [Hagen, 1973, p. 214]

My role is to introduce LMA as a creative resource, to offer ideas and to "hold the space" for the explorations that follow. Prapto's reference to himself as a "gardener" is a fitting description of the atmosphere here, in which the students are provided with the conditions in which to grow, to embody their feelings and imaginings, to be inside themselves and to see the world from inside their individual and collective stories.

Themes that appear in almost every student questionnaire at the end of the year are those of the freedom they feel to explore, discover, and "fail", the exhilarating way in which imagination and body merge, and the acquisition of LMA as an invaluable tool. They are all able to recall specific moments, often from the earliest sessions, which vividly stand out. I see these as moments in which integration and transformation crystallized. There was no holding back, no part split off from total involvement in the moment. In these moments, the most profound education has taken place.

# CHAPTER THREE

# On the meaning of the body from a psychoanalytic perspective

"There is little in the practice of psychoanalysis more perplexing (or more interesting) to me than the question of how experiences in analysis facilitate the healthy development of the patient's sense of being alive in his or her body. In health, the experience of being bodied and the experience of being minded are inseparable qualities of the unitary experience of being alive.

(Thomas Ogden, 2001)

I t is primarily those aspects of psychoanalytic theory that pertain to the preverbal stages of infancy which seem to me to be most significant for the development of thinking about movement as a psychophysical process. It is during this earliest period of life that movement (and its accompanying sounds) comprise the primary means of both communication and affect regulation. In this chapter therefore, I look to these elements of psychoanalytic theory in particular, in attempting to illuminate the dynamics of these primitive communications.

## Preverbal communication

If preverbal communications can be received and responded to by parents or carers, then all will usually be "good enough" (Winnicott, 1971) in the baby's earliest environment; however, if these primitive communications consistently fail to be received and responded to appropriately, or, indeed, if a baby is hyper-sensitive and difficult to soothe, the infant may resort to various extreme measures to deal with the felt lack of attunement and containment.

Psychoanalytic theory has described with great specificity the ways in which infants unconsciously develop and communicate their anxieties; and recent work in the field of neuroscience appears to substantiate much of this thinking, by confirming the long-lasting effects of early psychophysical patterns being encoded in the brain.

Using British object relations as my primary framework, I would like to draw out some of the major themes used to describe infantile psychological and emotional experience in a way that sheds light, either explicitly or implicitly, on the integration of the psyche and the body. Object relations theory explores the complexities of human relationships, the dynamics of change that occur both within and between individuals in response to the turbulent interplay of opposing forces—of love and hate, or absence and presence, for example—starting from the very beginning of life.

In this chapter, I draw on aspects of the literature that support the integration of the physical sensory level of experience within the psychoanalytic framework. The underlying intention is, on the one hand, to think about how drawing out these particular aspects of psychoanalytic thinking can enhance the theoretical underpinnings and the practical working methods in the field of DMT, where there has been sustained interest in a psychodynamic framework (Dosamentes, 1990; Lewis, 1979; Pallaro, 1996). On the other hand, I will be considering whether and in what ways a synthesis of these aspects of psychoanalytic theory with the theory and practice of movement might broaden the scope for accessing and integrating patients' primitive, preverbal experience in psychotherapy. Although "the talking cure" is not short on theory about this stage of development and its ongoing effects throughout life, one wonders if there may be room for development in the area of technique as regards the incorporation of bodily, sensoriaffective experience into the practice of psychoanalysis and psychotherapy.

It seems that psychoanalysis has often associated bodily sensation with that which cannot be brought to the level of thought—either a retreat into one's own world or an escape into physical action. Even though Freud had initially emphasized the core link between body and psyche, it almost seems that, until the impact of affective neuroscience reversed the trend, there had been a progressive movement in psychoanalysis away from thinking about the body and towards the analysis of thought that was somewhat disconnected from the body. Freud was concerned with the meaning of genital experience; Klein emphasized the relationship with the breast. Bion, as a key post-Kleinian, emphasized thinking, bringing the focus further up the body, so to speak, and into the head. Seen this way, the focus of attention has risen upward over time, from lower body to upper body to head! Although I will discuss later how it can be said that bodily experience is implicit in Bion's theoretical framework, the focus of his work has, perhaps, been more on thinking about thinking than thinking in any direct way about the body.

Developmentally, the non-verbal language of movement and affect precedes verbal thought—though it is accepted that non-verbal "thought", referred to by Woolf (1965) as infants' "alert inactivity", is present from the beginning. The task, it would seem, is not only how to restore access to this primitive language, but, equally, how to find the means of translating the primitively based psychophysical experiences into words. As I turn to a review of some relevant theory, perhaps it will be possible to consider how a synthesized psycho-physical perspective may offer a means of addressing this task. Winnicott (1971, p. 131) articulates the challenge of being able to "verbalize without insulting the delicacy of what is preverbal, unverbalized, and unverbalizable except perhaps in poetry".

## Relevant psychoanalytic theory

### Beginning with Freud

To begin at the beginning—Freud himself famously wrote that "the ego is first and foremost a bodily ego" (Freud, 1923b, p. 26). From this we can understand him to be describing the self as primarily a bodily based entity, but perhaps not actually seen as separable from the mind and emotions. His early work on hysteria was to involve him in deriving meaning from a range of physical symptoms; this work led him to observe that bringing about a change in thinking could effect a change in the expression of the symptoms. Although the bodily ego was thought to derive its energy from unconscious "primary process" activity—physical instincts seeking immediate gratification—the fact that body and psyche are interconnected seems to have been clear to Freud. That the body can reflect unconscious processes is certainly true, but that it, like dreams, can also participate in bridging the unconscious and conscious realms has perhaps still not been fully explored.

Freud discovered that the best method for eliciting unconscious material was "free association", the process of thinking aloud, giving voice to all thoughts without censorship, the premise being that everything that occurs to the patient during the session has relevance for the analysis. Because non-verbal, bodily-felt experience is integral to patients' affective states as well as to the overall atmosphere of sessions, might the emphasis of free association be slightly rebalanced to take more account of this material? It may, in my experience, either support or contradict what is being verbalized.

Child psychotherapy, as developed by Melanie Klein and her colleagues, allows for much more freedom of movement through its use of play, thus providing greater scope for incorporating non-verbal expression into the free associative process. In the "play technique", Klein observed and interpreted symbolic activity in children's play, thereby elaborating on Freud's understanding of the unconscious. Non-verbal physical communication clearly contributes to the intuitive response of therapist to patient. I wonder whether, if attended to, dwelt in, so to speak, more fully by the therapist, the bodily expression might be seen to offer even greater insight into children's unconscious phantasies. Might intuition come to be seen as deriving from bodily based phenomena?

A couple of random excerpts from Klein's *The Psychoanalysis of Children* follow, and may serve to illustrate how she "read" and made use of non-verbal communication. She gives powerful descriptions, trusting, as in fiction, that the reader can grasp the meaning without providing detailed analysis of the body and move-ment as experienced in the transference and countertransference. And yet, as the training in psychoanalytic infant observation has shown, there is often added meaning to be obtained from a more detailed and specific level of description of non-verbal behaviour.

". . . her attitude towards me was very mistrustful and reserved. She only became more lively as she began telling me about a poem which she had read at school" (Klein, 1932; 1989 edition, p. 59). I find myself curious to know what specifically Klein noted in the non-verbal behaviour that conveyed the mistrust, the reserve and the liveliness.

"Obsessive brooding and a curiously unchildlike nature were visible in the suffering look upon the little girl's face" (*ibid.*, p. 35). Here again, whether a more detailed description of what specifi-cally was noted in the non-verbal behaviour that conveyed the "obsessive brooding", the "unchildlike nature" and "suffering look" would help enlighten the reader is perhaps a moot point. Readers will no doubt create their own picture of these children's behaviour, but how precisely it resembles what Klein actually saw is unknowable from the data.

## The internal world

According to Klein, primordial mental activity is created out of an "amalgam of sensory, somatic and imaginal experiences" (Likier-man, 2001), which are object relational from the start. One of Klein's major contributions was to describe the way an *internal world* is formed through processes of *introjection* and *projection*, based on primitive phantasies about what comes in and what goes out of bodies. Relationships with real parental and other figures are inter-nalized, as are relationships with *parts* of these objects, most notably with the breast. The internal world is experienced as a real psychic space inhabited by "internal objects". These mirror but are not the same as real figures in the external world, as they have become imbued with the child's own mental impulses. Primitive oral and anal phantasies about these objects and relationships with them constitute and colour much of the infant's experience, according to Klein.

In speaking of an internalized object world, Klein is obviously not intending to describe an actual bodily space; nevertheless, the psychic internal world will have *real* effects on and in the *real* body and these will be reflected in posture, gesture, facial expression and patterns of movement. The ways in which movement dynamics are used to express and/or defend oneself—the relationship to time, space, weight, and flow, as described in Chapter Two—will be influenced by the atmosphere and relationships within the internal world. These dynamics may reflect archaic patterns formed in infancy. Alvarez (1998) calls for thinking of the internal world in terms not of its population by static objects but rather in terms of the "movement of thoughts . . . their location in space . . . their position in time". She borrows the term "temporal shapes" from developmentalist Daniel Stern (1985) to describe the dynamic qualities of internal objects.

*Internal characters, roles and scenarios*

It seems to me that internal objects, much like characters in a play, can be said to each have their own distinctive complex and contradictory physical and emotional characteristics. They are not only recognizable as voices in one's head. The ways in which these internal figures come into contact with one another create unconscious psychodynamic patterns that can be thought about in both interpersonal and intrapsychic terms.

As stated, the neuromuscular and autonomic nervous systems encode patterns of early object relations, so that there may be "long term autobiographical memory of a pathological internal object relation" that becomes the unconscious working model (Schore, 2001a, p. 68). Because the body plays a key role in affect regulation (through the inhibition of breathing or the tightening of musculature, for example), its significance would seem to be central in the study of primitive psychic states. It seems to me that having access to an experiential language like LMA could be of help in deciphering these states and bringing them to consciousness.

*Unconscious phantasy*

Klein described the earliest creation of symbolic meaning and imagination as "unconscious phantasy"—(she used the "ph" spelling as a way of denoting the unconscious nature of the images and thoughts). She discovered through her work that these phantasies were often bound up with thoughts about the contents of her patients' own and/or their mothers' bodies. Totton (1998) comments that, although Klein was body focused, she was not speaking about the "fleshy body", but about the body as it existed in phantasy. I think this view overlooks the basic premise that real physical sensations are at the root of phantasy. "Physical experiences are interpreted as phantasy object relationships . . . a baby in pain may feel itself as being hated" (Segal, 1991, p. 20). A bodily event is experienced as a psychological one, and vice versa. We can see the impossibility of separating the one from the other. But Totton may be right in his implication that the literal body might be largely left out of the analytic process.

> One patient in movement therapy found it nearly impossible to move out of a slumped upper body posture, the same posture she remembered always seeing in her depressed mother. Much as she would like to do something else, her identity was linked to her felt experience of being adhesively stuck to a particular internalized image (or shape, as Stern suggests) of mother. Another patient, who had experienced an inappropriately intrusive father, spent the beginning of sessions taking charge of the space—opening closed windows and curtains, or closing opened ones—and finally placing herself uncomfortably close to me. Without saying a word, she very effectively showed me what it felt like to bear being colonized by an intrusive object.

I am interested in discovering the many ways in which, as well as taking up residence in the psyche, unconscious phantasies and internalized object relationships become represented in the body and its patterns of movement. It would seem that, if not recognized, psychobiological patterns may unknowingly be handed down from one generation to another, liable to impinge upon attempts to develop one's own separate identity.

## Splitting and projective identification

The first and primary relationship is between the infant (in particular its mouth) and its mother's breast. In Klein's view infants create primitive phantasies about the breast based on their physical and emotional relationship with it. These unconscious phantasies are derived from what can be thought of as a psychophysical relationship with this "part object". Klein described the defensive mechanism of "splitting" of the breast, and later the mother herself, into a separate idealized, good version of the object and a persecutory bad one. This representation took root in the patient's internal world as well as the perceived world of external reality, and laid the ground for what Klein later described as the "paranoid–schizoid position". Splitting, by providing a way of maintaining a sense of order and of keeping chaos at bay, was seen by Klein to be a normal part of infantile life. It could also be thought of as a defence against the anxiety associated with separation. The patient's own ego could also become split, which, as Klein described, commonly resulted in narcissistic qualities like omnipotence, denial of dependence or difference, and mania.

It is in phantasy that the infant splits the object and the self, but the effect of this phantasy is a very real one, because it leads to feelings and relations (and later on, thought processes) being in fact cut off from one another (Klein, 1946, p. 6).

At times the splitting of the good and bad breast/maternal object and/or self, may have a loose parallel relationship with the splitting of body and mind. "Cutting off painful thoughts and feelings is the same as interrupting feedback loops in the body which tell the body (and the brain) about itself" (Carroll, 2002, unpublished manuscript). In other words, one form of splitting might describe a defensive mechanism in which the infant exists in a disembodied mental space, quite dissociated from uncomfortable, perhaps unbearable, physical sensations.

In order to keep unbearable feelings at bay, physiological steps are taken to disengage from experience. The infant may muscularly bind or freeze the flow of feelings, as if defending against the ordinary effect of gravity, or contrariwise, feel gravity to be so great a force that it depresses or deflates the body into a lifeless, de-energized state. Babies who have experienced trauma are seen to stare into space with a glazed expression. Although seemingly passive, these babies are probably expending a great deal of energy in keeping unbearable feelings outside of their awareness. In Schore's words, hyperarousal still exists underneath dissociation, but it is "anaesthetized" or "numbed" (Schore, 2001a). (It would seem that in other cases, what appears to be passive *hypo* arousal is indeed just that, a baby who has seemingly given up on making contact.) Klein (1946) called the practice of ridding oneself of unwanted (or sometimes prized) parts by unconsciously projecting them into another "projective identification". The term denotes a kind of wholesale transportation of unwanted parts of the infant (or the infant within the adult) into the mother/carer/therapist. Schore states that "projective identification represents not linguistic but mind-body communication" (Schore, 2001a, p. 67).

Bion extended the meaning of projective identification by explaining that if the mother can receive (that is, embody, digest, and return) her baby's projections, then the communication has an adaptive rather than defensive, function for the infant. The baby can take back his feelings, processed and made bearable by mother's empathic response. However, if this is not the case, if mother is not able to receive the projections and process them for her baby, then the projective identification becomes a defensive mechanism, an evacuation or splitting off of unbearable feelings.

In thinking about the psycho*physical* effects of splitting and projective identification, I would say they describe attempts to rid oneself of contact with both mind *and body.* How do we understand the effect on a baby of projecting a part of itself into its mother? And what is the effect on the mother? The loss of parts of the self can be thought to create a vacuum within the infant, which exerts a pull, an intense need to be filled. The mother is subject to this pull and if not able to process the projection, she may be at risk of being pulled into and taken over by the infant's agonizing distress. She may create her own psychophysical defences against the pressures of being "pulled"'.[1] Although Bion did show us that an aim of projective identification may be to communicate with the object, we know from Klein (1946) that it may also be intended to control or intimidate.

In projective identification the experience of loss and depletion are implicit. In what ways might such a phantasy manifest on a body level? Genevieve Haag (2000) observed that it can express itself as a split between the two halves of the body—upper/lower, right/left, or back/front—as if the good half, is kept for oneself, the other is denied and projected outwards. Or there may be a sense in which a particular part of the body has been unconsciously colonized by a "bad" maternal object. Haag (*ibid.*) observed that separation can be experienced as a loss of part of the body.

> A patient found it impossible to move her lower body as she sat, legs outstretched and welded together. Her arms, meanwhile, freely created elaborate patterns in the air, which accompanied her verbal description of having joyful feelings as she arrived for her session. In the counter-transference I felt her aggressive and sexual feelings were felt to be dangerous, and were split off and projected into me, making me feel like a dangerous male predator.

> Another patient [who is described in Chapter Eleven], seemed to represent a damaged internal object in the left side of her body, while the right side, which could perform difficult and daring movements, represented a determined but at times bullying internal object. The dynamic tension that can occur when body halves recognize the existence of each other was explored in movement therapy.

## Further links with neuroscience

Schore (2002) links projective identification with dissociation, a defence against traumatic experience concerned with fundamental body-based functions. Dissociation is characterized by immobility and carries the emotional tone of helplessness and hopelessness.[2] As already explained, when early traumatic experiences are encoded in the nervous system, there is an initial response of hyper-arousal which, if not contained, is followed by dissociation. The hyper-arousal belongs to the sympathetic nervous system and is experienced as physical as well as psychic pain. Dissociation belongs to the parasympathetic nervous system, which is below the level of conscious control. There is, Schore states, always this sudden switch from hyper-arousal to dissociation. It seems as if the neural circuits become overloaded and the system relies on this fail-safe mechanism to maintain its sense of integrity.

## Depressive position

The ability to bring the disjointed parts of the self back together, to recognize that the breast/mother is only one object/person, not two, and therefore contains both good and bad elements is described by Klein as the "depressive position". Here, the omnipotent or manic defences against catastrophic anxiety that characterize the paranoid–schizoid position and the narcissistic preoccupation with self, in which unacceptable parts of the self are rejected, give way to *concern* for one's primary objects, both internally and externally. There is greater tolerance for ambivalent rather than split feelings and for acknowledging both internal and external reality.

The implied softening of the defensive processes that keep parts separate would seem to suggest a relaxation of the body, both the neuro-musculature and the breathing, an acceptance of one's relationship to gravity and an ability to tolerate the mixture of feelings and sensations constituting one's own inner depths. I am not, however, suggesting that having a relaxed body necessarily implies an achievement of "depressive position functioning". It is more complex than that.

I would suggest that this process of re-incorporating parts of oneself and moving towards the "depressive position" may be a gradual process rather than a case of being either in one Kleinian position or the other. Kleinians clearly point out that there is seen to be a constant fluctuation from one position to the other throughout life. I wonder, however, if even this idea of fluctuation does not fully describe the less clear middle ground that characterizes the process of change.

It seems to me there is a process of gradually working these rejected parts back into the whole personality to the degree tolerable from moment to moment; and perhaps movement, through its discrimination of fine adjustments in response to stimuli, can be of help in containing this process. It is understood, I think, that the effect of such reincorporation of parts may not always result in feelings of heaviness and lethargy associated with depression. Sometimes parts may return with feelings of aggression and/or a robustness of energy. Whatever the feelings, I think they will be accompanied by a sense of being more filled out and substantial.

In differentiating between the "paranoid–schizoid position" and the "depressive position", there is an implied change from a depleted, tense, or flattened two-dimensional surface sense of self, a "front", one could say, to a filled out three-dimensional being, supported by the introjection of a three-dimensional internalized healthy object. This offers the capacity for a different kind of object relationship in which the capacity to reflect on oneself while in relationship as if from a third position is possible; this is described by Britton as "triangular space" (Britton, 1998). This three-way relating, Britton postulates, has resonance with the triangular Oedipal drama as described by Freud. In acquiring a three-dimensional perspective and embodied sense of self, there is an implied mourning in the acceptance of separation.

## Symbol formation

Hanna Segal (1986), writing about one's capacity for symbol formation, considers symbolizing to be a three way relationship—between the symbol itself, the thing it stands for, and the person for whom the one thing stands for the other. It therefore has an affinity with the three-dimensionality of the depressive position.

> A patient describes a feeling of bearing a heavy weight on her back, which she has always carried. She begins to wonder who this weight belongs to; she takes a deep breath and stands tall, as tears roll down her cheeks. Another patient describes the way she leapt off a park bench when a policeman on horseback came alongside. Surprised by her reaction, as she is fond of horses, she realizes in the session that the horse seemed to recreate the dark looming shadow her father cast when he approached her in childhood, threatening physical harm.

Both Freud and Klein emphasized that words provided an alternative to bodily actions, which were not in themselves deemed symbolic; though, of course, Klein took account of children's play as a form of symbolic expression. In reconsidering the possibility of exploring movement and other sensory and perceptual experience as symbolic activity, I am suggesting that bodily expression need not be seen only as a defence against the mind; on the contrary, it may offer a way of contacting and integrating primitive unconscious phantasies, anxieties, and defences. The body has a powerful memory, and reflecting on the physical experience, finding words to describe it, can replicate the early interaction between mother and baby, when mother provides the verbal language to contain and describe the baby's non-verbal communication.

It would seem that both an over-involvement in sensation at the expense of the mind or an overuse of the intellect and verbalization disengaged from the body can equally militate against symbol formation. Both would tend to evoke something more akin to what Segal (1991) called symbolic equation, a term to describe a two-dimensional activity that cannot be understood by the person themselves to have symbolic meaning.

> A young man, after three months of weekly sessions, recognized that he had not yet dared to move. He filled every session with an almost non-stop stream of verbal narrative. Finally, he admitted to feeling uncomfortable always sitting in the same huddled position on the studio floor, his knees drawn up, feet on the floor, arms hugging his lower legs. Sitting alongside him there, I felt the anxiety he experienced in this very bound, compact position. Yet I felt that should I draw the focus of attention to his body too prematurely or too often, it would only exacerbate his frozen state. On this occasion, I encouraged him to speak about his thoughts/fantasies/feelings about what it might mean to move. He unhesitatingly said it would be sexual and he would feel humiliated. I suggested that I was perceived by this part of him as a voyeur, exploiting him, which he confirmed. This patient was equating any bodily movement, even a shifting of position, with sexual display or exploitation.

## Wilfred Bion's thinking about mental processes

It was Wilfred Bion who pointed out the ongoing normal oscillation (as distinct from a chronological progression) between the two Kleinian positions which carries on throughout life; he used the abstract symbol ps↔d to illustrate this dynamic fluctuation between a predominantly fragmented or predominantly integrated state (Bion, 1963). Betty Joseph (1989, p. 96) echoed this idea in describing the "minute movements of emergence and retreat" within a psychoanalytic session. I am suggesting that a more conscious attuning to the sensoriaffective experience by both patient and therapist offers an additional avenue by which these fluctuations can be tracked.

Many of the concepts Bion used to describe *mental* processes have, I believe, much to offer in thinking about *bodily* processes, and in fact, that the bodily experience is implied in Bion's very original thinking. I briefly describe a few of his concepts as follows.

His notion of a baby's innate "pre-conception" of a good breast, for example, conjures up a vivid physiological image of a baby who is wired up and ready to latch on and be filled and held.

It is interesting to consider the physiological dimension of the essentially mental process of engagement between infant and carer or therapist and patient which Bion described as containment. I think containment also has meaning in terms of the complex somatic and emotional responses that are at the heart of non-verbal communication and projective identification. Is empathy not, in its most basic form, a bodily based relationship, in which sensoriaffective as well as mental experience is communicated? Houzel (2001, p. 45) evocatively describes the container as requiring both (maternal) elasticity, and (paternal) firmness—this speaks of an openness to absorb the other person's condition, while maintaining contact with one's own bodily structure and position.

Purely linguistic communication, disconnected from a sensoriaffective base, calls to mind the "knowing about" (−K) which Bion distinguished from the deeper experience of "knowing" (+K); the latter implies a knowing from the inside that could be said to be beyond words or, at least, not limited to words. These terms also resonate with the qualities of two and three-dimensionality discussed earlier—"knowing" implying a three-dimensional embodied experience. This can be said of Bion's "alpha function" as well, which he described as referring to a mental space (of mother's mind, for example) in which the raw, unprocessed *sensory* material, termed "beta elements", could be contained and transformed by thought.

From a movement analysis perspective, it seems quite possible to imagine the process of *containment* Bion describes operating in an opposite direction—that is, when words and thoughts are used as a defence against feelings, they could be transformed into an alpha function experience by a sensoriaffective containing, which would promote the embodiment of thoughts, and thus a three-dimensional *knowing*.

Bion (1963) describes the "attacks on linking" one thought with another that emerge when there is felt to be no trustworthy container for one's projections. Again, in movement terms, I wonder whether this phrase of Bion's might usefully describe not only the inability to link thought to thought, but also thought to sensation to affect, back to thought, etc., the ability to link up different levels of experience—physical, mental and emotional, intra- and inter-personal.

Bion's concept of "O", which seems to describe a complete, almost spiritual surrender to the unbounded universal sense of open-endedness, seems to suggest a sense of safety in experiencing "unintegration" which, according to Winnicott, resembled the formlessness of the infant's original state. This basic trust in a genuine feeling of support would seem to imply a bodily letting go.

The seemingly polar opposite state to that is "nameless dread", in which the infant feels the life-threatening terror of a lack of containment; it calls to mind the feeling of "disintegration", characterized by a terrifying feeling of catastrophic chaos and lack of holding. This powerful experience also reflects something of the complex physical component of real and imagined, internal and external, object relations.

## Metaphors or descriptions of reality?

Images that refer to the body or physiological processes are frequently used to describe psychoanalytic processes; yet it is not always made clear by the authors whether these images are purely metaphorical or whether, and in what sense, they are describing real physical or psychophysical processes. Even if we assume that images that conjure up physical processes—such as Bion's "containing" or Winnicott's "holding"—are meant purely metaphorically, would it not be helpful to contemplate the meaning of these images in terms of real sensory experience? Are we meant to be able to use the metaphor to evoke an experience that is partially rooted in the physical domain? I do not mean to imply that this question is ignored in psychoanalytic literature; it is often addressed directly through discussion of clinical work.

A vivid example of such a metaphor in clinical practice was given by Judith Edwards in an article titled "On being dropped and picked up" (Edwards, 2000), in which she describes her work with adopted children. Edwards writes, "After the half-term break he zoomed back into the room and deliberately dived off a chair straight onto his head." As is discussed in Chapter Seven, a similar physical metaphor, that of *falling*, is seen to represent the emotional experience of three-year-old Anny.

The poet searches for metaphors that will convey a fresh way of representing something, that will, hopefully, have resonance on more than one level. We are invited to mobilize the metaphor as a means of enriching our understanding—sensorially, viscerally, emotionally, mentally and/or imaginatively. Metaphors used by psychoanalysts have indeed provided a way of integrating and embodying these different domains, of providing a means for shifting dynamically from one level to another in a way that draws together different aspects of self experience. It must be assumed that the meaning of the successful metaphor will be registered in the body as well as in the mind and feelings.

*The second skin—a powerful metaphor*

Psychoanalyst Esther Bick (1968) observed that the actual skin contact between an infant and its primary carer supports the baby's sense of identity and feeling of containment. Bick described the extreme means a baby uses when there is a felt absence of containment (of Bion's "alpha function"), when the baby feels he has to hold himself together in the absence of a good object and in the face of the extreme terror of "nameless dread". The various coping strategies Bick observed involved the development of what she called a "second skin". Examples of this were the baby's use of rigid muscularity and bodily stiffening, or a fixed gaze that latches on to something inanimate as ways of holding itself together. Other examples might be the holding of breath or closing down of the senses. The term "second skin" has even been used to describe the use of precocious talking as a way of self soothing.

I think there is much that can be explored in tracing and unravelling the remnants of these primitive psychophysical phenomena as they enter conscious awareness in a therapy setting—the sensations of overly tight (or flaccid) musculature, which may subtly fluctuate from moment to moment, from body part to part, reflecting a possible range of co-existing psychological and emotional associations. It could be suggested that in some cases these long held and deeply embedded second skin processes represent an unconscious narrative of their own which run parallel to a more usual psycho-analytic exploration of mental thoughts and images. Even though they are rooted in primitive attempts to block the flow of feeling in the body for protection and defence, the archaic second skin phenomena may be awakened and potentially transformed.

Donald Meltzer (1975b), Frances Tustin (1990), and many others have built on Bick's work in their treatment of severely disturbed and autistic children, for whom the sense of having an intact body is impaired or non-existent. They observed patients unable to project or introject, because both processes require at least a semblance of three-dimensional spaces of container and contained. They were often seen to overuse physical sensation as a way of dealing with their lack of capacity for real object relations; their repetitive or ritualized movements seemed to be generated not as a means of expression but as a means of basic survival—movement, in this case, as second skin. They were observed to have a tendency to metaphorically *stick* to objects in an echoing or mimicking way as a desperate attempt to quell catastrophic anxiety.

Tustin describes the following example:

> . . . an autistic boy . . . as the end of the session drew near, in order to feel that we were one and the same and that we were not sepa-rate from each other, would imitate the way I was sitting. He would place his legs as my legs were placed, and his arms as my arms were. As I interpreted this in relation to the coming end of the session, he began to accept the fact that we were separate and different, but not disastrously blown apart. Gradually, he began to be able to be "born" as a separate individual in his own right. [Tustin, 1990, p. 67]

Tustin and Meltzer referred to this lack of spaces, replaced by flat surfaces as *adhesive identification*. Having no feeling of bodily space of one's own, safety is sought in sticking to another, perceived as a spaceless surface. Without a sense of one's own three-dimensional body space, there cannot be a conception of an object's three-dimensionality. This is perhaps true not only for the very disturbed, but for most people from time to time—when, by dissociation or splitting, one loses a sense of having one's own centre of gravity or axis, one attempts to restore a sense of reality by "sticking" to or over-identifying with others. Suryodarmo also describes this phenomenon, calling it "sticking", being "glued" or "fitting" together in relationship as opposed to seeing and allowing oneself to be seen, from and in one's three-dimensionality.

*Other spatial metaphors*

Donald Meltzer (1981) considers the ways in which primitive phantasy, the core material of psychoanalytic enquiry, is based in passionate erotic attachment to parts of the body—to association with internal spaces of the mother's body, namely the breast, the head, or the rectum and/or vagina. These bold ideas, so bodily based, clearly conjure up more than unconscious *mental* processes. The *claustrum*, as Meltzer terms the tendency to be mentally locked into an association with part of the mother's body, is another example of a metaphor that bridges the domains of the psyche and the body. He describes the phenomenon as a "geographical psychosis" which manifests in a patient's distorted picture of the world in which he lives or is imprisoned (*ibid.*, p. 477). It would seem that "listening" to the sensoriaffective experience, which goes with the territory of perceived seclusiveness, might help to gain perspective and a route out of the claustrum.

Anzieu (1989) speaks of the formation of a *psychic envelope* which, like Bion's container, protects the psyche. If its containing function is weak, it is said to be broken into by holes (Anzieu, 1989, p. 102). He makes clear that he is not speaking literally about the mechanics of the interrelationships between psyche and soma, but that he enjoys engaging with the affective power of the metaphoric description.

*Transitional space*, described earlier as a term coined by Winnicott to designate the area, for the baby, between being psychically merged with its mother and relating to her as a separate being. It is associated with the imaginative realm and the child's ability to be lost in play (Winnicott, 1971). It would seem, therefore, to be located between the Kleinian positions, or perhaps more accurately, between Segal's "symbolic equation" and symbol formation.

## The Winnicottian perspective

In his thinking about the ways in which catastrophic anxieties in infancy can lead to a disruption of psychophysical integration, Donald Winnicott's work resonates closely with that of Esther Bick. One way he described the *false self*—which, like Bick's "adhesive identification", is characterized by imitation and compliance—was "living through a mind or intellectual life which has become separated off from the psyche-soma" (1949).

Winnicott was quite explicit in his thinking about the body's psychophysical nature, stating that a satisfactory relationship between the psyche and the soma is inherent to integration. He writes repeatedly about it: ". . . the inherited tendency of each individual to achieve a unity of psyche and soma", the ". . . indwelling of the psyche in the soma"; and "The basis of psyche is soma, and in evolution the soma comes first. The psyche begins as an imaginative elaboration of physical functioning . . ." (Winnicott, 1988, p. 19). Whereas Meltzer and Tustin draw attention to the almost addictive use of bodily sensation as a mindless retreat (as observed in their work with autism), Winnicott seemed to emphasize conscious bodily awareness as integral to the "true self".

The body, in Winnicott's view, was the very container for a three-dimensional sense of self. He wrote about the precariousness of this container, using the image of a bubble, whose equilibrium could be upset by impingement from outside; the membrane of the skin separating ME from NOT-ME can easily be disturbed (Winnicott, 1988)—Kleinians would say the equilibrium could be upset from the *inside* as well as the outside. Either way, the image is a dynamic one, implying movement, adjustment and change, not unlike Bion's image of oscillation between ps↔d. But whereas Bion's image lends itself more to the workings of the mind, Winnicott's speaks of something that has its basis in bodily experience:

> The true self is bound up with bodily aliveness. It comes from the aliveness of the body tissues and the working of the body functions, including the heart's action and the breathing. . . . The *spontaneous gesture* is the true self in action. [Winnicott, 1960, p. 147, my italics]

Winnicott's work, therefore, lends itself naturally to further investigation of the body and movement as a therapeutic resource.

"Unintegration", in Winnicott's view, could be desirable, as it implied a feeling of being safely held, thus allowing for the possibility of relinquishing the need to hold oneself together. I linked unintegration with Bion's concept of "O". Perhaps the language of movement could support a way of navigating the internal world which could more clearly differentiate between the three different conditions—*integration*, in which all the parts are felt to make up a whole; *disintegration*, in which parts are felt to be missing or disconnected and lacking in substance; and *unintegration* in which the parts are allowed the freedom of release into a trusting but unknown relationship with the environment.

## In the footsteps of Winnicott

Winnicott's colleague Marion Milner was a key figure in developing the relevance of her own as well as her patients' bodily experience in her practice. She explored filling out her own three-dimensional "body attention" during sessions, and stated, "I was beginning to believe more and more that what I said was often less important than my body–mind state of being . . ." (Milner, 1969, p. 42). She was interested in "the free play of unplanned expressive movement", which she describes as "contemplative action" (*ibid.*, p. 263). Her work is explored further in Chapter Four in considering the somatic countertransference.

Joyce McDougall's interest in the psychophysical domain is primarily in decoding the "mute and mysterious messages contained in psychosomatic processes" (McDougall, 1989, p. 31). She asked, "How are we to 'listen' to them? And how eventually may we hope to render them symbolic and thus communicable through language?" (*ibid.*, p. 43). McDougall is interested in finding the routes towards enabling these symptoms to be felt and thought about, and thereby to enter the triangular space of symbol formation. Like Bion's image of transforming unmentalized sensoriaffective material by the conversion of beta elements into alpha function, McDougall strives to transform psychosomatic symptoms into something that can be integrated and made "thinkable". She is, therefore, incorporating the language of the body into the analysis.

"Perhaps body language", she writes, "is the only language that cannot lie" (1995, p. 157).

## Summary: the body in psychoanalysis

I have described how primitive defences, psychophysical in nature, get employed in infancy to cope with what can be experienced as overwhelming or catastrophic anxiety if the earliest relationships are felt to go wrong. These defences or "protections" (Mitrani, 2001), which can even become established prenatally, may result from actual early trauma or extreme privation, or they may be resorted to by overly sensitive or premature babies who may be prone to traumatic infantile experiences. The outcome of these early traumatic experiences is ". . . a crippling of the emerging elemental state of subjectivity and the gradual development of true objectivity" (Grotstein, in *ibid.*, p. x).

In this chapter, I have tried to draw out those elements of psychoanalytic theory that seem to have strong resonances with the bodily felt experience, that which has its basis in infancy, but which continues to live on throughout life. By allowing bodily felt experience to become a more conscious part of the analytic relationship, might it be possible to reinvest the metaphoric imagery used to define theory with its original meaning, to perhaps even enhance the original meanings? In psychoanalysis, because the adult patient is usually on the couch, movement *per se* is limited, but bodily sensation, if attuned to, is certainly not absent.

Might language to describe preverbal states arise naturally as a result of therapist and patient more consciously embodying their psychophysical states? Perhaps, at times, material needs to be communicated and received on a purely non-verbal level. Perhaps not everything can be put into words; as Suryodarmo puts it, to receive *"in-formation"* via the body can itself stimulate *transformation*.

DMT also stands to be broadened and deepened by the substantial theoretical material provided by psychoanalytic thinking, which so vividly articulates the mechanics of primitive psychological processes. Bodily experience, whether in movement or stillness, is interconnected with phantasies and feelings about object relations.

In looking at the two fields separately, it seems clear that their areas of interest are mutually supportive, if not precisely the same. Assuming that, to some degree, consciously or unconsciously, physical sensory experience is a dimension of all experience, the body must be seen to be an essential locus for registering meaning. The evidence from affective neuroscience is convincing: emotional experience is inseparable from the body. In the next chapter, I will concentrate on the relevance of the sensoriaffective bodily realm in any therapist's own experience of the countertransference.

## Notes

1. Suryodarmo used the terms "pulling and being pulled" and "absorbing and being absorbed" to define the unconscious processes that make for unclear communication in movement practice.
2. It seems important to mention that, although Schore makes an enlightening link between the two, not all dissociation includes projective identification.

# CHAPTER FOUR

# Embodied attentiveness:
# a synthesis of frameworks

"The emergence of some of the most primitive levels of
psychic and body-ego experiences in the patient can depend
on the body–ego perceptions in the analyst . . ."

(Milner, 1969)

W hat I call *embodied attentiveness* is the ability to engage
with psychophysical states in a way that enhances the
therapist's ability to attune to that which may be felt but
is not yet thought or verbalized, akin to Bollas's "unthought
known" (Bollas, 1987). When Milner refers to "body–ego perceptions in the analyst", she is talking about analysts' direct experience
of their own bodies as a means of registering what is being trans-
mitted non-verbally by their patients; this material is absorbed by
the analyst through the unconscious process of projective identification. As Milner suggests, the therapist's rebalancing of attention
to include awareness of the sensoriaffective realm facilitates the
patient following suit; in much the same way, the patient learns to
develop a mental space for reflection as a result of being contained
by a thinking therapist.

I am suggesting that the body and its movement offer a language that expresses and reflects the earliest stages of development and the nature of patterns rooted in primary relationships. In this chapter, I look at the theme of countertransference from various perspectives, and consider, in particular, how therapists can enhance and refine their awareness of the somatic aspects of countertransference.

I am interested in how psychophysical experience is transferred from patient to therapist, and how therapists may develop their ability to *read* and *receive* patients' bodily experience through strengthening their ability to be attentive and responsive to their own. In my view, the more the therapist is anchored in his body, aware of the sensations and feelings, the breathing, the relationship to time and space, the more likely he may be to consciously introject patients' anxiety rather than react to it.

## Primitive communication

The most primitive communications—which have their origin before words are available and during which time the body itself is the primary site for all experiencing and communicating, all introjecting and projecting, all proto-thoughts and feelings—can find their way into any therapy setting whenever these preverbal states are aroused, usually through projective identification. These processes are often unconscious for both patient and therapist. The patient may be quite cut off from bodily and/or emotional experience, and yet strong feelings may still be stirred in the therapist/analyst.

Quinodoz (2003, pp. 103–104) argues that although patients' *feelings* are absorbed by analysts, there does not tend to be recognition of their own or patients' accompanying *bodily* experience. She writes:

> How can a newborn baby distinguish between the feeling of frustration and the overall bodily sensation that accompanies hunger? It is often these complex early experiences, in which bodily and affective aspects are confused, that the patient projects into the analyst in excessive projective identification. The analyst then

receives these early projections in the context of his adult internal world, and tends to translate them immediately into a more mature register. In other words, the analyst tends to experience the feeling directly, without paying attention to the bodily manifestations that accompanied it, because he immediately unmixes the affective and bodily aspects, seizing only on what seems to him most valuable— that is, the feeling, at the expense of the bodily sensation that merely ushered it in.

. . . the analyst needs to listen out not only for his own affects, but also for the bodily manifestations accompanying both his affects and his bodily fantasies. . . . It may be the analyst who feels in himself the bodily experience that accompanied the patient's unconscious affect, in which case he will be able to help the patient attend to this sensation, to progress from the sensation to the bodily experience, and thence to its emotional meaning.

Of course it cannot be taken for granted that a therapist can *know* what a patient is feeling solely based on the countertransference—but it is possible to form hypotheses that can be checked out with the patient when deemed appropriate. It seems to me that by slowly building recognition and tolerance of bodily processes, as they are integrated into the work of therapy, the ability to think and speak about them develops naturally.

It can be said that this non-verbal level of communication is always present, and underlies verbal communication. I am suggesting that the bodily aspect of the countertransference may be a primary mode of contact, especially when patients need to be felt and contained on an infantile level, and are unable to communicate verbally or to symbolize.

## *The verbal and the non-verbal*

The interrelationships between the body and language are complex. On the one hand, Stern has written about the potential rupture words can create between the verbalizing and the experiencing self (Stern, 1985). Concurring, Pally warns that "by privileging verbal communication, psychoanalysis accentuates this rupture and sacrifices the understanding of states that cannot be verbalized" (Pally, 2003, p. 73).

On the other hand, words can clearly be seen to contain emotional experience, to provide meaning. This view conveys the essential purpose of psychotherapy. As Margaret Rustin puts it, "Words can build bridges over the unbearable discontinuities of our infantile emotional experience" (Rustin, 1998, p. 444). Satyamurti draws attention to the power of words to symbolize experience, drawing a parallel between the use of language by the poet and the psychoanalyst—they "share an acute attentiveness to the precise and multiple meanings and associations that words may have, and to the way [words] are transformed by the specific contexts in which they are used" (Satyamurti, 2003, p. 32).

Some question whether that which was experienced before access to words can be reached by the use of words. Bion suggested using a broad definition of *language*, "to include behaviour of which it is sometimes said 'actions speak louder than words'" (Bion, 1970, p. 125). In part, what I am investigating here, is the interrelationship between verbal and non-verbal languages—the way in which "nonverbal behaviours and visceral responses unconsciously shape language, and language unconsciously shapes nonverbal responses" (Pally, 2003, p. 89).

It would seem that in order to avoid words being used defensively, either to distance from experience through intellectual abstraction or to evacuate experience through "verbal diarrhoea", they need to reflect or spring from a depth of feeling contained in the sensoriaffective level. Ogden (2001, p. 9) has drawn attention to "the moment prior to speaking . . ." which, he writes, "is not a moment of affectless waiting; it is a moment alive with desire, the impulse, the need to give voice to the inarticulate."[1]

## Countertransference

Since the seminal paper by Paula Heimann (1950), countertransference has become increasingly recognized as being of prime importance in the work of psychoanalysis. Nowadays, it is central to psychoanalysts' work to include the feelings and thoughts aroused in them by patients' projective processes, as they take in and contain unconscious communication. Countertransference is no longer, as Freud originally thought, something that hindered the analytic process.

This taking in and containing implies more than a mind. The patient's material is taken into a three-dimensional bodily container where it *in-forms* the therapist. LMA, supported by Amerta Movement, may offer a way to help render the "minute movements", as perceived within the transference and countertransference, less mysterious and more decipherable. Countertransference "is a signal— just a signal—that needs to be decoded" (Rosenfeld, 1992, p. 83).

*Somatic countertransference*

Although it is certainly true that "feelings" can be said to bridge bodily and mental experience, and psychotherapists are, therefore, implicitly including the body, the question still arises as to whether the therapist's ability to recognize and endure the patient's material, to differentiate its properties from the therapist's own internal processes, would be strengthened by the therapist developing her own sense of embodiment—her awareness of the quality and the location of her own sensoriaffective experience. And, if so, could this process be augmented by (*experiential*) familiarity with Laban's framework for describing movement "vocabulary", by giving names to what may previously have been felt intuitively but not named?

Turp, in exploring similar questions about "unconscious somatic communications", writes, "With the refinement of vocabulary comes an enhanced sensitivity.." and the ability to "distinguish more and more nuances . . ." (Turp, 2001, pp. 180–181). Through recognizing one's internal sensory experience and one's relationship to space and time, one can, I think, make the absorbing of others' emotional states more conscious.

It seems to me that paying attention to bodily experience in any therapy setting, and thus making it part of the work, may invite projective or adhesive identification to be brought out in a more conscious and direct way. Both parties can experience it tangibly, phantasies can be recognized and when appropriate, named and interpreted. The role the patient ascribes to the therapist (Sandler, 1976) can be felt through the body. Sandler describes the act of "role-responsiveness" as a "process of dynamic interaction".

It would also seem that by developing their own sense of inner spaciousness and stillness of mind and body, therapists could help themselves in *preparing to work* with patients. Suryodarmo suggests that in order to be able to "read" and respond to another person, or even a landscape, one starts by feeling one's own skin; then one can see, and only then can one "read". Marion Milner described this state as "expectant stillness" (Milner, 1969).

Equally, I have found that paying close attention to my own bodily experience in movement or stillness after a patient leaves allows me to recognize what I have taken in. In this process of digestion, I can more clearly feel the nature of the patient's internalized object or part of the patient that has been projected into me. It is through giving them form through movement that essential qualities of the transference and countertransference become more recognizable. Laban Movement Analysis can be used at a later stage, to reflect on the somatic countertransference, particularly on tracing patterns that emerge, and change, over time.

*Somatic countertransference in body psychotherapy*

In investigating what has been written on the subject of somatic countertransference, I found that the phrase is not much used in the psychoanalytic field, but within the field of Reichian derived body psychotherapy it is common. Michael Soth writes that the concept of somatic countertransference is equivalent to saying "swimming fish" (Soth, 2002). The body is the element within which his work is "rooted".

Roz Carroll (unpublished manuscript, 1997) says that it is our capacity to resonate with others that is harnessed in the use of somatic countertransference. She writes of an "involuntary imitation" of energetic states, which can be made conscious and amplified, and ultimately given meaning. The principle expressed in many healing traditions, both East and West that "subtle energy"—energy fields, energy centres, energy pathways—represents the unconscious in bodily form, is a fascinating discussion that, though clearly related to this discussion of somatic countertransference, is unfortunately beyond the scope of this book.

I would say, however, that the concept of energy, in my view, is closely related to Laban's concept of flow; and I go along with Laban in thinking that the element of flow (of energy or breath or movement) implies a relationship to feelings. One way of working with energy in my practice of movement psychotherapy is through the recognition of a dynamic created between opposing forces inside the patient, or within myself in the countertransference. These inner conflicts can be experienced physically as patterns of congested or potential energy in the body, often coloured by deep feelings; movement can provide a vehicle for exploring subtle changes in these patterns, which can be recognized both intra- and inter-personally.

I very much agree with Soth and Carroll that the bodily countertransference is rich with meaning. It is on the question of *how* the body is brought into the therapeutic frame that my approach seems to differ. Various "bodywork techniques" may be employed as part of body psychotherapy (according to a body psychotherapy website). The implicitly more active, directive role taken by a therapist seems to me to militate against working with transference and countertransference in the tradition of psychoanalytic object relations, in which the patient, via free association, takes the lead and brings the material. I believe this issue is actively being grappled with as "new dimensions in body psychotherapy" are forged (Totton, 2005).

*Listening with the whole body: the contribution of Marion Milner*

Marion Milner was a pioneer among psychoanalysts in consciously cultivating her "body-mind state of being" in sessions (Milner, 1969, p. 42). She wrote that the "direct sensory (proprioceptive) internal awareness . . . the actual 'now-ness' of the perception of one's body" could be equated with "perception of oneself". She described the way in which the deliberate sinking into her internal perceptions, without looking for correct interpretations, often seemed to allow interpretations to "emerge spontaneously" (Milner, 1960). Milner clearly recognized the value of what I am calling "embodied attentiveness".

A disciple of Winnicott, Milner linked her appreciation of "direct body awareness" with "the mother's loving care of the infant's body" and thus saw it as part of the "facilitating environment" (Winnicott, 1971). Parsons (2000, p. 26) writes that Milner's distinctive contribution to psychoanalysis was to "help analysts listen with their whole bodies and not their ears alone". Milner recognized that it was not only a mental space that she cultivated as a therapist, but a bodily space as well; and that this bodily container was not simply passive, but was actively receptive.

## A synthesis of frameworks—aligning Laban Effort qualities with psychoanalytic thinking

In order to think more deeply about countertransference processes, and as a way of synthesizing material drawn from movement analysis (Chapter Two) and psychoanalytic thought (Chapter Three), I will describe the affinity of certain psychoanalytic ideas with one or more of the four basic elements which motivate movement, as defined in Laban Movement Analysis—*flow, weight, space,* and *time*. In doing this, my aim is to further explore how this particular alignment of the two contrasting perspectives on human experience could facilitate the recognition of meaning in the mainly unconscious non-verbal communication that exists within all therapy relationships.

### Laban's links with Jungian theory

Laban's four Effort elements have affinities with different realms of human experience. Around 1950, Laban discovered Carl Jung's papers (Jung, 1921) delineating the four functions through which, Jung suggested, humans make contact with the world—feelings, sensation, the intellect and intuition. According to Jung, these four "functions of the ego" describe the means by which "consciousness obtains its orientation". "Sensation tells you that something (tangible) exists; thinking tells you what it is; feeling tells you whether it is agreeable or not; and intuition tells you where it comes from and where it is going" (Jung, 1961, p. 219).

Although I am exploring links between LMA and object relations theory, not with Jungian ideas, I feel that the natural affinities Laban saw between his basic Effort qualities and Jung's "functions of the ego" are helpful in establishing the realm of experience correlated with each of the movement qualities.

In this synthesis, flow has an affinity with (emotional) feeling, weight with (physical) sensation; space with thinking, and time with intuition (see Chapter Two). When considering how to demonstrate the possible alignment between psychoanalytic ideas and Laban's Effort framework, I find that, although it is impossible to separate and compartmentalize the psychoanalytic ideas and the experiences they describe as being exclusively to do with one of the basic Effort elements, it is possible to use these four elements as a loose framework for organizing a discussion, and for thinking about the involvement of one or more Effort qualities in various kinds of object relationships, as well as noting the absence of the others.

In Laban terms, one might say that DMT emphasizes the element of weight (the physical sensation) and psychoanalysis emphasizes space (the mental perspective). The principle of achieving an integrated state by cross-modal or multi-modal perception—engaging through one mode of perception, and "translating" this perception to other modes (Stern, 1985)—underlies this exploration into making links between the two methods for promoting personal growth.

### Internal and external worlds: the Effort qualities revisited

Although internal and external experiences are never totally distinct, it can be said that, broadly speaking, Laban's elements of weight and flow, together comprising the "dream state", reflect the internal world of sensory and affective experience. The elements of time and space, together comprising Laban's "awake state" could be said to pertain to the outside world. The former pair of elements is more associated with "being", the latter with "doing"; the former in Suryodarmo's language would be related to the *organism* and the natural world, the latter with *organization* and the realm of imagination and thought. Over-involvement in either direction may indicate a defensive psychic structure. If the former can be said to be predominantly about self experience, and the latter about experience of the outside world, then it is the interweaving of the two which will support dynamic object relationships.

It is arguably impossible to separate out one element from the Laban vocabulary—to say that only flow, for example, is present in an infant's movement, when we can readily observe the baby has weight, and moves in space and time. One can consider which movement qualities could be said to (consciously or unconsciously) describe one's *predominant* motivation, either from moment to moment or over time; and one can describe the conjunction of different realms of experience the movement qualities denote.

LMA can provide a way of describing strengths, weaknesses, and changes of state. Psychoanalyst Schwaber has written about the "depth of information to be illuminated in attending to *state* as an ongoing physiologically rooted experiential and observable phenomenon, fundamental to a consideration of psychic process" (Schwaber, 1998, p. 668).

*Flow*

The element of Flow (designated as *free* or *bound*) is related to the control or freedom of feelings as expressed in movement. When there are failures in the primary environment, or when a baby is extremely susceptible to affective disturbance, the infant's reactions could be characterized as expressions of *bound flow*. By this I refer to strategies for affect regulation and control in the face of archaic feelings to do with the fear of extinction.

These defences may also involve the body in a tightening of the musculature, in which the element of *weight* is also engaged, unconsciously and perhaps prematurely, when the baby (or patient) instinctively feels that for survival, she must take on the responsibility for holding herself together.

The use of splitting to control painful or terrifying experiences may represent the early use of bound flow. Betty Joseph described a state of suspended animation between love and hate, a kind of on-guard paralysis serving as a response to the felt impending perils of the "bad" object (Joseph, 1989, p. 31).

Although Klein does not usually speak directly about the body, it would seem, according to the Kleinian framework, that one implication of the installation of a good internal object is that it reduces the need for an overactivation of bound flow and a premature involvement of the musculature for protection.

These primitive feelings, which I have linked with the element of flow, are not confined to infancy, of course. The early failures of the infantile environment leave their imprint to some degree on everyone's later experience; but if they were a persistent, significant feature, they will be more likely to be restimulated in times of stress or trauma throughout life.

In Chapter Eleven, I describe how a young dancer deals with traumatic injury by accessing her strong will and determination. After a near-fatal car crash, she surprised the doctors by harnessing her use of weight, as well as her strong mind (Laban's space Effort), in order to regain the use of her body. In so doing she succeeded in keeping her overwhelming feelings of loss and terror at bay. In the course of movement psychotherapy, the experience of intense bound flow became self-evident; she was able to gradually let the flow of feelings enter her experience, allowing herself to grieve and tolerate the terror and anguish she had previously had to keep at bay. She discovered that this pattern of binding feelings in order to attain a kind of stability had actually had its origins in infancy.

*Weight*

Weight is related in Laban's analysis to the realm of *physical sensation* and thus also to *intention* or agency—what one wishes to do with one's weight. The quality of the initial relationship with the mother's body will establish a baseline for how the infant continues to experience his own body. The sites of greatest sensation and affect, the mouth, the lips, tongue, and the digestive tract, are all highly stimulated in feeding and digestion. And the skin, the body's largest and most vital sensory organ, can be thought of as the mediator of earliest communication. The sense of touch, the skin to skin contact with mother, writes Anzieu, gives rise to the experience of the ego (Anzieu, 1989, p. 97). He described the sensations of the body acting as a containing *envelope*, serving as a source of security and creating a grounded sense of presence through a cooperation with the force of gravity.

A conscious awareness of the body begins to dawn with the experience of separateness. I wrote the following in my first observation of baby Sam, who will be introduced in Chapter Five. He was one week old:

> . . . he drifted in and out of sleep, half opening his eyes sometimes, seeming to register mum's voice, and possibly her face and/or the light

from the window. All the while his fingers, especially those of his right hand articulated clearly and individually, finger by finger, unfolding and folding in, occasionally involving the lower arm. There was a beautiful clarity about his hand movement. His left hand also explored, extending into space beside him, as if delicately feeling the air.

This kind of gradual dawning of sensation (and perception), as if just beginning to recognize the nature and potential of embodiment, can also happen in later life, when there is a "thawing" of frozen emotional affect (Lechavalier-Haim, 2001). If there has been a premature interruption in the natural development of the early flow and weight based relationship between mother and baby, it can impose lasting psychophysical damage. As has been stated, neural pathways laid down in the first months of life establish the foundation for all future experiencing.

*Disturbance of relationship to flow and weight in autism*

Tustin, Alvarez, Meltzer and others have drawn attention to the heightened sense of emotional arousal in some types of autistic children, as if the brakes could not easily be put on the intensity of the free flow of affect. Bound flow is either not accessible or is resorted to in the extreme in an attempt to block out the emotional onslaught. In the former case, it is as if the flow of feeling cannot be controlled and embodied, as if there is no experience of a body with weight. In the latter, weight is used in the service of the kind of muscular tightening described by Esther Bick. Neither represents a true embodiment of the sensation of weight. Those with autism sometimes create repetitive, ritualized patterns of movement which, at first may seem to involve the elements of weight and time in their use of rhythm; in actuality they attempt to obliterate any relationship with the reality of time or with the outside world of space in an attempt to regulate the tremendous flow of unmanageable feelings. Physical sensation is used as a kind of retreat.

As well as the defensive use of ritual in autism, Alvarez describes an autistic patient who expresses a lack of relationship with the body in another way. He has no ability to *articulate*, she says, either physically or mentally. "It was a long time before he discovered he had bones, muscles or joints in his body, or power, will or freedom of choice available in his mind" (Alvarez, 1992, p. 26). She describes another patient's "progress toward the development of intentionality", which was gained slowly through the therapist's observing and remarking upon each "hint of a gesture or movement". This picking up of tiny signals conveyed by physical action seemed to enable the patient to gradually build and tolerate a sensory physical body, and thereby gain a sense of both purpose and agency. This patient was beginning to *embody* her sensations and feelings and it would seem that this provided the basis, the home ground, for beginning to embody her mind.[2]

*Weight and flow: Laban's dream state'*

Could Laban's *dream state* (weight and flow) support the therapist/analyst's capacity to bear painful affect, to receive and contain such material when the "psychic skin" of the patient is underdeveloped? Could the dream state be thought of as akin to what Bion characterized as *reverie*? Does the ability to BE in relationship precede the ability to THINK in the relationship?

It is perhaps the rare moments when both inner and outer experience are simultaneously embodied that characterize deepest integration, and in which change can actually occur. The felt experiences of weight and flow can be embodied in a right brain to right brain (or heart to heart) contact; then the left brain, versed in the language of time and space (Laban's "awake state"), can find the words to think about the experience, to, as Bion has said, "make the thought thinkable". Suryodarmo referred to such moments of embodiment as "crystallization", saying they form the basis for transformation. This seems to resonate with Bion's thinking about what constitutes knowledge (+K) or "alpha function", which seemed to combine sensoriaffective and cognitive experience.

*Space*

In Effort theory, Laban associates the element of Space with attention to the outside world and to the realm of mental awareness; one's focus is deemed to be either sharp and *direct* or broad and *flexible*. The need to relate is at the core of human experience. Without an experience of space, engaging in relationship is not possible.

(Equally, it could be said that without an experience of one's body, there is no point of reference for the experience of space and the movement of the mind.) In object relations, the internal and external object worlds of both patient and therapist come together in the therapeutic space. This involves a complex picture, which as Meltzer described it, implies spaces inside both the self and the internal objects, as well as inside the external object and its internal objects (Meltzer, 1960, p. 39).

Winnicott's "transitional space" denotes the negotiation of separateness, and is the area where symbolization and creativity are born out of confronting the experience of loss. Winnicott speaks of transitional activity as play; in this sense it seems to describe a mindful involvement in bridging the inner experience of weight and flow with that of time and space—the sensoriaffective with the relational. Rey has described the interim period on the way to autonomy as a "marsupial space" (Rey, 1988). This image could usefully describe a therapy relationship.

Play is an activity involving exploration to investigate the various possibilities of positioning and proportion between the experiences of connectedness and separateness. An overextension of one's sense of space lends itself to omnipotence; a shrinking of one's space may imply feelings of persecution or claustrophobia, or worse perhaps, the lack of interest in "being in space" at all, which could be described as complacency or mindlessness. This is a theme that I think can be explored with depth and subtlety by attending to non-verbal experience.

In Chapter Six, baby Sherry finds the experience of external space and time perplexing and often persecutory. In Chapter Ten, the adult Beth experiences a deep nostalgia for an idealized state in which she and mother shared an emotional cocoon characterized by depression.

*Orientation in space: dimensionality*

Laban's other body of theory, Space Harmony, concerns one's *orientation* in space. It too is mutually compatible with ideas from object relations. Psychoanalyst Rey states that "primitive thought is centered on the first moves taken by the infant to structure space" (Rey, 1988, p. 229). The following affinities between Effort qualities and spatial dimensions have been noted by Laban and others; I think these can provide food for thought about the meaning in one's orientation to space:

- The *vertical* dimension is linked with *weight*, gravity and grounding. Suryodarmo describes its affinity with the classic feminine principle, the qualities of "staying" and receptivity.
- The *horizontal* dimension is linked with *space*, widening or narrowing one's perspective, one's point of view. Kestenberg emphasizes its relational nature by calling it the feeding dimension (Kestenberg Amighi, Loman, Lewis, & Sossin, 1999).
- The *sagittal* dimension (forward and back) is linked with movement through *time*, and thus with mobility, with "going" or "doing". For Suryodarmo, this has an affinity with the masculine principle.

Laban further described two-dimensional planes, each of which have a primary and a secondary dimension, and therefore, a missing third dimension.

- The vertical or *"door" plane* denotes a steadfast quality; it lacks the sagittal dimension associated with time.
- The horizontal or *"table" plane* lacks a vertical dimension, and thus challenges one not to lose one's own (vertical) axis in the attraction to space and time.
- The sagittal or *"wheel" plane* lacks a horizontal dimension, and thus gives a feeling of intentional rolling on or holding back, undeterred by spatial concerns.

Each plane, then, has an affinity with a different state of mind— stable, awake, and near states, respectively (see Chapter Two).

*It will be helpful for the reader to explore the three planes and the effect on you of aligning yourself to space in these different ways. Imagine the door, wheel, and table, each from the perspective of your own body.*

When three-dimensionality is weak, it can be useful to note which dimensions are most accessible to someone, and which one tends to be least accessible. In Chapter Six, it is clear that baby

Rodney, who dashes through the space, oblivious of his surroundings, uses the "wheel" plane in order to cope with anxious feelings;
whereas baby Alice has a weak sense of her relationship to gravity
and her own vertical axis. She seeks refuge in a world of time and
space, the horizontal plane, sometimes clearly confusing an imaginary world with that of here and now reality.

In psychoanalysis the concept of dimensionality has been used
slightly differently, that is, to describe different qualities of emotional functioning within both the internal and external worlds,
which also have implications for the relationship between therapist
and patient. In three-dimensionality there is the sense of whole and
separate objects interacting. There is an implied sense of volume or
"triangular space" (Britton, 1998), making it possible to reflect, and
to integrate one's perspective with one's experience.

Two-dimensionality, following this line of thinking, implies a
lack of psychic space and an inability to think. Although both
perspectives speak of two-dimensionality, it has a more pathological quality in psychoanalysis than in LMA.

## Time

In line with the Jungian model, Laban associated the element of
Time (accelerating in *sudden* time or decelerating in *sustained*) with
intuition, having a sense of timing, a felt relationship to impulse,
rhythm, phrasing. In psychoanalytic object relations, one thinks of
the timing of communication, the therapist's intuitive decisions
about when to make an interpretation, the patient's challenge to
follow "the unconscious logic of sequence" in free association
(Bollas, 1992, p. 48). In this sense time is not only objective and
external, but is related to internal impulses associated with memory
and desire. In "working through", there is a rhythm of advance and
retreat; there may be cycles of stagnant repetition.

Betty Joseph describes this shifting as crucial in terms of
patients' need to maintain "psychic equilibrium" as they reconcile
new perspectives with old systems of defence (Joseph, 1989). The
timing and associated meaning of changes from state to state are
always noteworthy.

The beginning and ending of sessions, and the gaps for holiday
breaks, challenge patients to endure absence in relationships, and

thereby recognize that reliable patterns can be established over time. This was illustrated famously by Freud's description of his nephew's game of "here" and "gone" with the cotton reel toy (1920g) in which both space (here and there) and time (now and then) were explored.

Even before the first intake of breath, a lifelong rhythmic undercurrent begins as the neonate responds to the sounds of the prenatal environment. Trevarthen has observed the way mother and infant "adjust the timing, emotional form and energy of their expression to obtain intersynchrony, harmonious transitions and complementarity . . ." (Trevarthen, 1993, p. 57). Psychoanalyst Monique Meloche writes, "If one's time is negated or denied, then the complaint may be of some negation of oneself, of feelings of unreality. To whom does time belong? To mother? Did she take it away when she left . . .?" (Meloche, 1988, p. 10). Patients deprived in this way find it difficult to be in the here and now.

The element of time for patient and therapist implies the possibility of movement and change, impulse and spontaneity. In movement psychotherapy and in child psychotherapy, where actual movement is part of the setting, time can be embodied; rhythmic expression can catalyse and support change. Initiation of movement, pause, hesitation, speeding up, slowing down, stopping, simply being "in time", when linked with thoughts, images, feelings, can be experienced as intensely as a dream. Time can, of course, also be used defensively in these settings, as a way of escaping being in the present by, for example, proceeding faster than one can think or feel.

Suryodarmo's notion of *being in* time means being in the present, in body, time and space "WITH one's memories AND desires" (to misquote Bion). Daniel Stern writes that "the present moment" is "never totally eclipsed by the past nor fully erased by the future. It retains a form of its own while being influenced by what went before and what comes after" (Stern, 2004, p. 31).

### Patterns of change as seen through the LMA lens

Child psychotherapist Margaret Rustin describes working with two young boys, who, in different ways, made her feel as if her "back was against the wall". She writes about how the situations changed over time. I would like to think about the changes in terms of movement dynamics. The first boy was wild and unpredictable in sessions, making Rustin feel helpless, as if she had no resources. She was made (allowed herself) to feel as "totally overwhelmed" as the boy had felt in his earlier life. She noticed that, "If I was 'firm', he would get genuinely panicked" (Rustin, 2001, p. 276).

It seemed that the boy and Rustin together devised an activity that contained and transformed this potentially violent atmosphere. The boy began to move the heavy furniture, enlisting Rustin's help. What, in Laban terms, had begun as an unruly expression of free flow and sudden time, often with strong weight put to the service of impulsive and sadistic manoeuvring in which Rustin felt the full force of terror in the countertransference, was transformed into a harnessing of strong weight, a focusing direct attention in space and an experience of sustainment in time—a *pressing* action—in which this boy began to feel his own power to take charge and shape his world, in cooperation with and assisted by Rustin. By gaining his agreement that the furniture would have to be put back in its original place by the end of the session, Rustin nurtured an acceptance of reality in terms of how much control of space and time was possible. The destructive use of free flow was channelled; the energy was harnessed toward something productive and safe.

Of the second boy Rustin wrote, "He was capable of almost complete lifeless inertia, sitting as if in a timeless world without movement or sound . . ." (*ibid.*, p. 280). Rustin described this as evoking either "empty-mindedness" or pressured, aggressive feelings in the countertransference. She recognized that the latter pushed her patient further away. She endured the intense loneliness alongside the boy.

In Laban terms, it could be said that she had to receive and contain a deadened or neutralized state without any movement dynamics; the communication that did transpire was non-verbal, a sharing of an internal state, perhaps most akin to the dream state in which sensation and feeling predominate, though here, even these elements were quite neutralized or unconscious; they were experienced by Rustin, however, as loneliness, and this was perhaps the catalyst for the boy's waking up. Rustin reports that he began to arrive on time, to glance at the clock, and there were "tiny moments of spontaneous activity".

Taking an overview in Laban terms of these two patients, one could describe the first journey as a move from mobile to stable state, and the second from dream to awake state (see Chapter Two). Of course, this does not mean that some states are "healthier" in Laban terms. One could imagine situations in which growth would be indicated by a move in the opposite directions. Any state can support unconscious patterns of defence. It is the rebalancing of Effort qualities (states) that can represent growth. It is the therapist's ability to receive a patient's state that allows the patient himself to recognize it, and to discover his own movement toward change.

## Summary

As John Steiner has stated, "the analyst is never able to be an uninvolved observer since he is always . . . enlisted to participate in enactments in the transference" (Steiner, 1993, p. 4). A therapist absorbs the atmosphere, the condition, the state created by the patient; the therapist is responsive to the role she is unconsciously assigned (Sandler, 1976). Much of what is being responded to is carried by non-verbal cues. Schwaber, 1998, quotes Jacobs (1994, p. 761), who writes that ". . . the exploration of the nonverbal dimension in analysis constitutes one of its few remaining frontiers. . . . it requires new ways of observing and new ways of thinking about what we observe".

In this chapter I have tried to further explore the overlap between the languages of psychoanalysis and movement analysis, to explore the benefits of their borrowing from, and making links with, each other, particularly with reference to the application of their potential synthesis in working with transference and countertransference. Object relations theory has a great deal to offer in underpinning and adding insight to the work in DMT, and it is my feeling that movement analysis may provide access to a "new way of observing", an embodied attentiveness, which can inform the work of psychotherapists.

The map (Figure 1) is an attempt to make a visual representation of some interrelationships between LMA and psychoanalytic ideas. A one-to-one mapping is not being suggested. Rather, I am

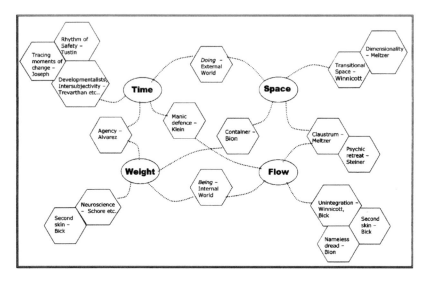

*Figure 1.*  Mapping relationships between psychoanalytic ideas and Laban Effort elements

indicating the affinities for certain movement qualities with the various ideas. Those ideas with a strong relationship with two Laban elements—such as claustrum and psychic retreat, both of which are primarily defined by space and flow—are linked to both. The synthesis of the two languages will be further explored in practical contexts when it is applied in Part II to observational studies and in Part III within clinical movement psychotherapy practice.

## Notes

1. I have explored the use of sound as a form of communication between the non-verbal and the verbal, most often with drama students, but also, if the occasion presents itself, with patients in movement therapy.

2. An approach to dance movement therapy based in LMA that has proved useful in working with autism was developed by Veronica Sherborne (Sherborne, 1990).

# PART II
# PSYCHOANALYTIC
# OBSERVATIONAL STUDIES

# Introduction

K eeping in mind that psychoanalysis and movement psychotherapy have a shared root in the primitive, preverbal level
of experience—both view experiences of infancy and early
childhood as crucially formative—I have chosen to use a series of
four psychoanalytic observational studies of babies and young children in order to explore links between the two perspectives. I am
interested in whether the combination of psychoanalytic thinking
and LMA can help to deepen understanding of the following:

- how and why particular preverbal psychophysical patterns get
  established in infancy?
- what in the child or the environment produces patterns?
- what the agents of change are or might be?

The studies comprise two that were carried out as part of the
training in Observational Studies at the Tavistock Clinic—one of
Sam, from zero to two years, and one of Anny, from three to four
years. The other two were carried out subsequently, and the
subjects were groups of children roughly the same ages as the individuals in the previous studies. The aim of all four chapters in

Part II will be to describe issues and themes that seem to be expressed through the activity and the primary relationships of the children observed.

## How observational studies are carried out: the Bick method

Esther Bick developed the format for psychoanalytic infant observation at the Tavistock Clinic, where it was incorporated into the training for child psychotherapy as early as 1949. It has since been taken up as a standard part of such trainings worldwide. It is based in the direct observation of the infant and its carers, the recognition, over time, of emergent patterns, and the recognition of the observer's own responses to what is observed. Infant observation has its basis in "the Kleinian understanding of the nature of early infantile anxiety, the requirement for containment of the fragile ego, and the mother's role as the prime container" (Rustin, M., 2002).

In practical terms, it works as follows. The observer visits the infant's home setting at a regular time each week; she does not try to be "invisible", but neither does she initiate any action. She simply observes and absorbs the effect of whatever happens within the allotted hour. (If the child is old enough to initiate contact with the observer, the observer responds in a natural way.) After leaving the setting, the observer writes detailed narrative notes, using ordinary language, of what she remembers happening during the visit, including the observer's own thoughts and emotional responses. There is a small seminar group which meets weekly, led by a child psychotherapist, in which one observer presents an observation for the group to discuss together in detail. Thus, each group follows the evolving narrative of four or five babies over the course of two years.

Excerpts from my notes made after each observation are displayed in smaller type, indented from the left, in each chapter. At times, the reader may wish to refer back to Chapter Two, where a fuller description of LMA is provided.

## The observer's role, the observer's experience

Infant observation requires the observer to be in a *receptive* state, which though seemingly passive, actually involves an active internal processing. It is a deeply involving experience, of which Sowa writes:

> [It is] not standing back and having a look, but it requires that one's entire being, one's identity as one has felt it is put to the service of a moment, and is opened to what pushes through and is as yet unknowable. [Sowa, 2002, p. 24]

This is related, I feel, to what I'm calling *embodied attentiveness*.

By allowing themselves to identify emotionally with both the baby and its primary carers, it is inevitable that observers' own infantile feelings may be stimulated by this close proximity to the preverbal states of infancy. It is now recognized that the presence of an observer usually affects the relationship between the infant and its carers in a positive way, by creating a separate "reflective space" (Rustin, M., 2002).

I would also say that the observer *holds the space*; this image implies a physical as well as a mental involvement, an embodied containing presence. If, as promoted by Suryodarmo's Amerta Movement, observers can experience their own three-dimensionality, their own position in the setting, and therefore more clearly absorb the experience of the subjects, there will be a more conscious reading of and attunement to the primitive "conversations". Put in Laban terms, the observer both experiences and perceives the Effort qualities of weight, space, time, and flow.

The way in which the observer takes in the scene, and the way she is viewed and used by the family, clearly prefigures the experience of the transference and countertransference of the clinician, thus making observational studies of this kind an exceptionally useful training tool. Because the observer plays an important role for the family, and because of the intimacy of the setting, transference and countertransference can be as present in infant observation as in clinical work. The difference is that an observer is not a clinician, and therefore the role does not include any attempt to effect a change or to verbally reflect back. Observation provides training in consciously absorbing and reflecting on material, as one experiences it, while re-membering it afterwards in writing notes, and in discussion with one's colleagues.

One question I am considering in regard to psychoanalytic observation is whether the perspective of movement analysis and the heightened bodily awareness and specificity it engenders, not only in being able to see and describe the subjects' non-verbal communication, but in recognizing the observer's own embodied sensory and affective experience, can be of use in augmenting what the observer gleans from the experience. I think it may do so, in part by providing an alternative language and categories for ordering the complexity of what is both experienced and observed.

This process of attending to and containing the "raw material" of infant observation—expressed in intimate preverbal "conversation" between infants and their carers—is undoubtedly a *psychophysical* experience. I think the material in the following four chapters illustrates how paying greater attention to the bodily experience of both the observer and the "observed", and considering the overlap of movement analysis with psychoanalytic ideas, have the potential to add to the experience of infant observation.

# CHAPTER FIVE

# One infant's manic manipulation of space and time

"I have attempted to introduce the concepts of space, movement and time as the basic elements, the weft and warp of
primitive human behaviour"

(Rey, 1994, p. 30)

In this chapter I describe my experience of Sam, whom I
observed on a weekly basis from one week to two years old.
I will try to convey something of Sam's struggle to come to
terms with various external events marking major life changes for
the entire family; these disrupted what might otherwise have been
an ordinary loving and secure start in life. I begin by giving a brief
description of the family and an overview of these events as they
arose during the two years I spent observing Sam in his home
setting. I provide excerpts from the observational material that
illustrate from a psychoanalytic viewpoint how Sam's internal
world was affected by the disruptions; and, using LMA, I describe
the ways his states of mind were reflected in his use of time, weight,
space, and flow.

## Background and overview

I first met the family two weeks before Sam's birth. Mother, father and three-year-old Pearl sat watching a game show on television as we chatted about the arrangements for the observation. They all seemed to be in a kind of stupor, eyes glazed and staring. This contrasted with the very lively decor of the flat and the fact that all three were very appealing-looking characters. I felt uneasy, as if there were hidden feelings in the air at this first meeting. Perhaps to liven things up,

> Pearl got up from the sofa and showed me a somersault, then walked across the room, with a limp, favouring a hurt knee. Mum and dad smiled at each other, as if acknowledging her attention-seeking behaviour in feigning a hurt. Physically, this did indeed appear to be the case, as Pearl seemed to be over-acting the limp, but I wondered if she may have been demonstrating how she felt inside.

I was to find out that mother's father was terminally ill, and he died when Sam was seven weeks old. The family spent a month away from London with Sam's grandmother. Soon after their return, there was an almost frantic momentum toward selling the flat they lived in, in order to buy another that was bigger. This was, as far as I knew, a very sudden decision that involved taking action quickly. Mother resumed smoking during this period, after having quit some years previously. Mother's ability to be present with her feelings of loss and grief seemed to go up in smoke, to be replaced by the intensive busyness and anxieties involved in the possible change of home.

The sale and purchase were completed, and the family packed up and moved in a very short space of time. The excitement of the move seemed to be short-lived. It was soon afterwards that the extent of dad's alcohol problem came fully into the open. Mother decided she would take the children and move out, even though dad agreed to attend Alcoholics' Anonymous (AA) meetings.

Mother was successful in finding a small flat that she and the children moved to straight away. This meant that Sam had had three homes in the space of his first year, as well as losing daily contact with dad. This presented huge challenges for Sam, and he seemed to react with manic defensive behaviour. In fact, unlike Pearl, who seemed quite depressed, both parents also seemed to cope through the use of manic activity. Because the family was reunited after six months and both parents were able to consider Sam's needs during the separation even though they were under much stress themselves, a greater sense of equilibrium was restored to Sam's world by the time the observation period ended. This equilibrium was notable in both his mental and emotional states and in his movement.

### Detail from observations

I will now provide excerpts from the observational material in a chronological sequence, discussing some of the psychological and emotional issues that seemed to arise in response to the various events. I will use a mixture of psychoanalytic theory and movement terminology (primarily LMA) to help think about the issues Sam faced and the choices he made in order to cope with a stressful internal as well as external environment. Attention to what Rey called the weft and warp of human behaviour—the basic elements of space, time and movement (the latter of which I choose to interpret as use of *weight* in the Laban framework) were crucial in thinking about what might be taking place in Sam's internal world as well as in external events.

In contrast to the manic patterns that would emerge later, I was struck in the first observations by Sam's relaxed and seemingly natural progressive negotiation of the new frontier of space outside the womb. At one week, I was particularly struck by the use of his hands as a bridge between his body and the space.

> Sam drifted in and out of sleep, half opened his eyes, registering mum's face and voice and the light from the window, while his fingers articulated clearly and individually, folding and unfolding . . .

rendering his perception from his own body's or fingers' "point of view". He seemed to experience his relationship with mum as still quasi foetal, himself as still felt to be contained inside her.

In his second week, the marsupial-type space he inhabited with mum seemed to include an increased use of the eyes. Vision, writes

Tustin, is the sense that acknowledges spatial separateness (Tustin, 1986).

> After about five minutes of my being there, he started to open his eyes occasionally, as though in a semi-conscious state, until he became more awake, his eyes finally staying open. Mum then picked him up and held him wrapped loosely in his blanket on her lap, his head in her left elbow joint. His eyes seemed to shift from one point to another in space—towards the overhead light, to the ceiling, to mum's face, which he seemed clearly to recognize as they focused on each other.

By 5½ weeks, Sam's sensual exploration and measurement of outside space as well as the more developed feel of his own body in motion were evident.

> He smiled at mum, looked at her as she settled him on the sofa, cooed at her. When she left him there, he moved non-stop, straightening and flexing his legs almost like bicycling, especially strongly through the heel of his left leg. His left arm extended out to the side and above his head, straightening and bending at the elbow. His right hand mostly stayed in contact with his belly; the fingers of both hands articulated. The movement seemed to be in conjunction with his taking in both visually and aurally. Sometimes I felt he was moving his limbs to the music of the video. Visually, he seemed drawn to the ceiling light and the bright yellow walls.

Sam's experience of his body in motion gave him feedback about both himself and the outside worlds. His simultaneous touch of space and self seemed to help sustain a harmonious balance between the two.

When Sam was seven weeks old, mum's father died after a long illness. Observations were cancelled for a month as the family was away. At eleven weeks, I felt that the slow and measured opening to the outside world witnessed in the first weeks began to show signs of strain. The family's sudden decision to put an offer on a larger flat depended both on another buyer's mortgage falling through and being able to sell their own flat quickly. Mum felt that though it was extremely stressful "the timing was perfect" as it offered a "new start" and took her mind off the loss of her father. She commented that she hoped that Sam was not much affected by events, adding that she thought it was easier being a second child.

*At eleven weeks (after a month off)*

Hearing my voice, Sam looked over from where he lay on the sofa and grinned at me. I smiled back, wondering if he could possibly recognize me. Mum said he laughed for the first time this week. It was when dad came home from work and kissed him all round his face and neck. Mum proceeded to do just this, nuzzling in close to Sam for several seconds, giving many quick kisses, during which he did briefly laugh. She said it's amazing how if Sam is happy, no matter how depressed she might be, she is infected by his mood, and the same thing if he's cranky.

Thinking in movement terms, the elements of free flow and direct focus in space are evident in Sam's initial state, as he lies contentedly on the sofa. When mum nuzzles him, she introduces an acceleration in time and, with her skin to skin contact, a light sensation of weight. Time and weight, which make up Laban's "near state", are opposite qualities to flow and space, which define Sam's "remote state". Mum seems to need to activate Sam, to make him more present for her (and perhaps for me too); as if his apparently calm observing presence on the sofa is not providing enough active stimulation or reassurance of his actually being there, being alive. It also seems to reflect her wish for, and delight in, physical closeness with her baby. In the seminar discussion of this material, there was speculation that Sam might be taking on a role of filling an empty space for mum, of buoying her up, of maintaining a lively atmosphere and providing the key male presence in the family, as there had already been oblique references to dad's problems regarding alcohol.

Mum's own anxiety and depression are dealt with in many instances by a hurrying through quality, hardly containing her highly emotional feelings and thoughts. Does she need Sam to join her in her speeded-up tempo and, at the same time, to provide the physical groundedness that mum lacks at the moment? In the following examples, I felt that Sam's relationships to space, time, weight, and flow were beginning to reflect his way of responding to mother's needs.

At 18½ weeks, near the end of the session, Sam was lying on the sofa where his sister, Pearl, was caressing him with what seemed and sounded like a difficult mixture of tenderness and pent up rage.

Mum came over and took Sam under his armpits, lifting him on to her lap briefly, then placing him on the floor, lying on his tummy and braced with his arms so his upper torso arced upwards. I had the feeling she wanted to show me his progress in this position. He supported with his hands, extending his legs off the floor behind him. He seemed to have a strong desire to move forward, but no way to do so.

At 21 weeks, there was a similar sequence:

Mum propped Sam on the floor supported by his hands, his fingers curled under like fists. Below his head was his toy with shiny balls floating inside. Sam looked intently at these moving balls and gurgled at them, moving his head nearer and further back; he was straining to hold himself up, until his head slowly weighed him down. He rolled on to his side and on to his back. This movement happened quite suddenly; he landed on his back and found himself looking up at the ceiling.

In these sequences, Mum seemed to want Sam to develop strength, to be able to use and support his weight; perhaps she was also interested in his having different perspectives. But what appears to be a push to have Sam mobilize his weight, rather than simply explore the physical sensations as he discovers his body in a more relaxed way, may again express mum's wish for him to develop quickly.

He then began to observe me observing him. I intently felt my whole body while watching Sam. Sam watched me intently too, his legs extended strongly with active feet pushing away through the heels and his hands and fingers stretched in space as we watched and communicated in this way. There was a very spacious feeling in my body and my mind, a feeling of mutual presence.

In his reflective interaction with me, his sensory and visual attunement seemed to be characterized by a sustainment in time and a freedom of flow, a lightness of weight and direct focus. The nonverbal communication had a meditative quality that seemed to derive from all the elements, weight, space, time, and flow being in a harmonious balance. There was a feeling of contact that seemed to derive from mutual psychophysical integration.

When Sam was twenty-eight weeks the family was packing for the move to their new flat. There were boxes all over when I arrived.

Sam sat on the living room floor with his musical-box toy in front of him. He seemed very happy, and totally unaffected by, or concerned about, the chaotic state of the room, the piles of things to be packed, and many boxes. He made squeals of delight throughout this observation. He hit his box strongly with whole arm movements, making the xylophone on top make sound.

He stopped as he watched dad tape a box, but showed no special feeling towards it. He then held his box so that it rocked back and forth towards and away from him, supporting it with his feet as well. Dad said Sam was now able to crawl, usually backwards and could get pretty well anywhere he wants to go.

In his deliberate use of strong physical actions and vocal sounds, Sam seems to be identifying with dad's sense of purpose and of being in charge. He is able to share the space with dad, but seems to also have an independent relationship to objects, as if firmly holding his own in the situation. This sequence on the one hand gives a picture of an appropriate involvement of father with Sam; but there is also a question about Sam's utter lack of disorientation in the chaotic space, and the whole scene as a kind of manic response to bereavement—taking control and quickly moving on. In movement terms, Sam's state of mind was predominantly "near", as he involved himself in the physical and rhythmic exploration of objects using weight and time. In this way, thoughts and feelings were kept at bay.

*Temporary accommodation*

Three weeks later, I was informed by mum that she and the kids were going to move again. I visited them in their temporary accommodation when Sam was thirty-two weeks. Mum commented that Sam wanted her with him all the time or he cried. His sense of events unfolding naturally in "space, time, and movement" in a familiar world was being interrupted for the second time. He did, however, find ways to orientate himself to the new situation. When he was sitting in his highchair in the new and unfamiliar kitchen, mum left him to tend to Pearl in her room.

Mum handed Sam a rusk before she left. Sam played at dropping the rusk to the tray and picking it up again. Then he looked at me, held the rusk over the edge and dropped it on the floor, then looked at me. I did not respond at first. He then turned away from me, began to squirm, looking towards where mum went. I picked up the rusk and put it back on his tray. He looked at me, mouth open, tongue out. I felt myself mirror him, and I felt we were in communication again. Later, when he almost cried, he put his head to his shoulder and I mirrored this too. There was clear recognition in him of being mirrored. Being in communication with the whole body in this way seemed to feel satisfying to Sam. It felt satisfying to me too.

Sam used my presence to support his exploration of something being dropped, and taken up again. We see a moment of doubt about mum's taking him up again when I hesitate before returning the dropped rusk. Perhaps his sense of being able to keep the attention of important objects in his world had sustained a blow by the new move. Dad no longer has the durability Sam may have come to expect.

In light of his insecurities, I felt he readily attuned to mirroring me as a reassuring confirmation of his being seen to exist. It could be said that he successfully got me to mirror him.

He seemed to be trying to get the measure of his new situation. In this excerpt he does this in a way that seems mindful, not manic. I was struck by the use of his tongue to explore the relationship between body and the outer space, seeming to affirm Bonnard's observation that "the first unit in the scale of measurement of experience is the tongue" (Bonnard, 1960).

But I also noted the beginnings of manic responses later in the session.

Sam took off, crawling very fast, making sounds to himself as he went. Once he called "dada" several times. His attention changed from moment to moment—near, far, always very excited. He has a habit of fast and audible breathing, like snorting, both in and out.

I wondered if dad's absence produced a mixture of responses in Sam, whether his feelings of loss were kept in the background by his identification with a "dad" presence. There seemed to be a mixture of anxiety and delight about phantasies of usurping the dominant male position.

At 9½ months, I observed Sam at the new flat where dad still lived. Though dad was present this time, I again saw a tendency for rather manic activity.

Sam crawled fast to the other side of the room and back to dad, pulling himself to stand, holding on to dad's legs as dad sat in his chair. He continued speedily round the room. "He's mad", dad said. I felt Sam looked drunk. Sometimes Sam would fall over to lie flat on his back. He would stay for a couple of moments, his attention glazing over, as if lost to the outside world. Then he would roll over and be off crawling again. This collapsing was very striking, as if he was reverting to early infancy for these moments.

This exaggerated sense of speed followed by a collapse was a pattern that I saw again and again. Sam was lacking any clarity of direction, propelled by anxious free flow and accelerated time in the mobile state, as if by keeping himself frantically on the move, he could avoid the reality of something having broken apart.

The aim of the defence of mania is to "annul a danger situation" (Freeman,1971). We could speculate that Sam may have felt anxious about the part he played in the parents' separation; dad's absence seemed to fuel omnipotent phantasies of annihilating and replacing him. The speedy mobility and changeability—the sense of going nowhere fast—that replaced the calm stability seen in Sam very early on, may have been used in an attempt to ward off feelings of guilt and/or fear of reprisals. At times, Mum seemed to contribute to Sam's overblown self image. At ten months one week:

Sam was standing, barely holding the sofa near Mum. Mum said "Walk, Sam". As if he was following her directions, he took three steps, in a sort of semi-circle, looking round his back toward Mum's direction or the telly on his third step, before sinking slowly to a squat. Mum said, "You walked!" Mum went to Sam, and said, "You walked! You walked! You clever boy!" He seemed delighted as if to say "Of course I walked; what's the fuss about?"

Sam seemed to feel pressured to be BIG. But rather than really embodying strength and balance, Sam seemed motivated by extreme bound flow and time, the mobile state again. Sidney Klein, in thinking about the emotional relationship to time, writes,

> ... the sense of time depends on the recognition of a pattern of repetition, which depends on a sense of the continued existence of objects and the emotional relationships bound up with them. ... The capacity to think of an object in its absence, to remember it and consequently to hope for it to reappear, depends on the tolerance of the feelings connected with its absence. [Klein, 1973, p. 6]

Sam's frantic movement seemed to be used more in aid of dispersing anxiety, evading affect, than embodying it. He had the illusion of holding things together through the speed of his movement. This could be thought of as a kind of "second skin" activity.

Sam's speed in crawling and push towards walking often gave me the feeling that he was unable to tolerate the confusing changes in his life. He seemed to deny the separation from father and instead seemed to phantasize having replaced him. His mental space represented a paranoid–schizoid split. Britton writes, "In the paranoid–schizoid mode the absent object is felt, not to be lost, but to be present as a bad or fearful thing" (1998, p. 142).

### The family reunites

It was no wonder, then, that when the family did reconcile and reassemble in the new flat, lovingly decorated by dad, Sam did not have an easy adjustment. Sam was one year and three months at the first observation after reuniting:

> Mum came down and answered the door. Sam was sliding down a few steps after her. He began to cry as he sat on the stairs, crawling up to the landing, then collapsing on to his front, crying, as mum passed him on her way to the kitchen. ... Once in the kitchen, Sam stood, as if wondering "what now". He stumbled on a cushion and fell, then rolled on to his back.
>
> ... Mum gave him a small cupful of cereal. He put the cup to his mouth as if to drink, then took one loop in his hand and ate it. Then he stumbled and spilled the cereal on the floor. There was no particular reaction to this.
>
> ... I went to find Sam and saw him climbing with hands and feet up the long stairway. He caught sight of me at the landing. He started on to the landing steps and let his weight go, lying flat, his left fingers lightly touching the vertical strut, his head on the step facing his hand.

He lay contemplatively for some time. I crouched in the landing space, and felt an emotional heaviness. He gathered himself in a quick burst and climbed on up, walking.

Suddenly finding himself in yet another new environment, the redecorated flat, in which his parents were reunited, seems to give Sam a feeling of dislocation. His response is to collapse and drop things. Is he feeling a loss of omnipotence now that dad was back on the scene? Is he feeling essentially dropped out of mother's mind? Or might there be a recuperative aspect to his collapse, as if there is a feeling of being contained in a safe enough space to finally begin to suffer some of his depressive feelings about loss?

What he now has to contend with is the real Oedipal dilemma, which is rather different from what he previously lived through. His striving to assert himself through accelerated time, has given way, in the collapsing, to a state of mind in which weight and flow predominated. The internally focused dream state—or, as in the last excerpt, flow, weight, and space, the timeless spell drive—are seen. He is giving in to, and experiencing, gravity. There is a poignant sense of melancholy in these moments of collapse, during which Sam seems to be affected by his new reality.

As he got used to the new arrangement, Sam showed evidence of normal Oedipal rivalry with dad in his love of lifting heavy things, handling the Hoover hose, and climbing to high places. He seemed keen to demonstrate his prowess to me. But these kinds of activities usually did not have the manic anxiety that his actions had in the rented flat. They seemed to be contained by the presence rather than the absence of dad.

> Sam climbed into a chair and then on to the kitchen table, standing in the middle of the table. He blew on two fingers. Mum said "hot!" and told me that Sam is showing me all his tricks and that last one, the blowing, made her sure of his intention to perform for me, because he hasn't done "hot" in a long time. He pointed at the photos of the family on the door. He said dada.

A member of the seminar group said she was reminded of Elvis Presley, hearing this last description of Sam. It was as if, with the family back together, Sam could play at triumphing over dad, without the level of anxiety previously observed, associated with wondering if he actually had. In the same session, I recorded:

> Sam ran through the space, twirled, ran back. I felt the sensation of the carpet on his feet delighted him; as did the room itself. Although excited, I felt Sam was not manic. I could see him clearly and he could see clearly. He seemed IN space and IN time, not driven by his frantic motion and emotion as in earlier times.

Sam seemed much more integrated, in the sense that his bodily and emotional expression were complementary and he shows himself to be alert to the space. His primary state of mind was probably awake (the object related combination of time and space), but he seemed to be enjoying the physical sensation of his body as well and a joyful free flow of energy; he seemed to be using all the movement qualities and firing on all cylinders. Omnipotence had been transformed into genuine potency.

When actually in dad's presence, a much more contented aspect of Sam emerged at times, a willingness to be little and able to learn. At sixteen months and three weeks:

> Dad asks Sam if he'd like some milk. Sam stands. When asked again he says yes. He comes near dad, beside the fridge. He seems to want to be up where dad is, taller than his height; but he seems to see the impossibility and he sits on his small stool.

> Dad starts to exit with the bottle, saying, "Come in here." Sam seems happy to have understood dad, and follows him. Dad says, "Sit down", and Sam sits on the velvety sofa. He takes the bottle from dad, and rubs his cheek on the velvet, lounging comfortably, turning his body once round. Dad exits, and Sam drinks vigorously and non-stop from the bottle.

Dad's containing presence seems to help bring Sam down to size, to settle into the experience of being contained inside his own skin. The soft pillow is a reminder of a good maternal presence. Dad, in mum's absence, seems to provide both a maternal and paternal presence.

I do not want to give the impression that once the family was reunited, the tendency towards manic activity disappeared. The tendency was there from the start in this family, in mother, father, and Sam. Each of them sped ahead to avoid dealing with the issues of bereavement in mother's case, addiction in father's, and separation in Sam's. It was difficult at times to be in the here and now.

As Bion pointed out, there is always an oscillation between depressive and schizoid tendencies throughout life as we manage to cope with life's stresses. As the observation period drew to a close I noticed the pattern of striving to be big and fast alternating with a sense of being collapsed and small. The development of a middle ground did not yet appear to be firmly established.

On one occasion, at nineteen months,

> Sam climbed triumphantly on to a kitchen chair and fell to the floor, hitting his head, opening a wound made earlier when he fell to the floor from Pearl's top bunk. I drove mum and Sam to the doctor for examination.

The persistence of a pattern of sudden collapse in time, space, and weight/movement, seemed to bear witness to the sense of extreme vulnerability that continued to characterize Sam's internal world. At 21½ months,

> Sam got up and put his head to the floor as if to do a somersault. He looked at Gran. She said, "We're watching." He put his head to the floor again, then looked at her. She again said we were watching. He then sank to the floor as he'd done earlier, spread out on his back with eyes closed, looking sad. He soon got up and climbed into the chair with Gran, who cuddled him.

I wondered whether I represented a sinister, persecuting figure in Sam's internal world then, one who demanded manly acts of daring which often failed and ended in collapse. Sam could not organize himself to engage in the physical action he envisioned. A mood characterized by flow and space (the rather disembodied, emotionally based remote state) interrupted his action which would have necessitated engaging in weight, space and time all at once.

## Summary

The manic defence was adopted by Sam as a way of surviving the psychic upheavals presented to him during the first year of life. He is seen to regress to the same kind of behaviour during his second year when internal or external anxieties are present. We could speculate that this primitive coping strategy had been laid down in Sam's psychoneurobiological patterning as an innate response to stress, which might endure throughout life. But we could also see there were times when Sam relaxed his protective defences as his environment became more positive.

The fact that, though his parents were dealing with emotional stresses of their own, they could usually receive Sam's projections boded well for his future. Therefore, his internal objects were more representative of life than of death, of love than of hate. By the time the family came back together in a mutually shared space in which triangular space was possible, I had every hope that feelings of "the presence of loss" would be possible. The natural unfolding of events in time, space, and movement would return to Sam's life.

# CHAPTER SIX

# The infant's language

"I knew the infant's 'language' but also knew the adult's. I was still 'bilingual' . . ."

Daniel Stern (1985)

In this chapter I draw on material from observations I made over a six month period in a playgroup for infants (under eighteen months old) and their mothers. A range of psychoanalytic themes and an accompanying range of movement dynamics were expressed within the different mother–infant dyads as each pair conveyed its own stirring narrative. In describing their "stories", I will again be exploring the possible benefits of interweaving movement analysis and psychoanalytic thinking.

The group met in a rather small but cheerful, toy-strewn room in a community centre. There were a few chairs around the perimeter where mothers would sometimes sit. Otherwise they sat on the floor with the babies. There were between two and twelve babies present at any session. This was a drop-in group, so attendance was somewhat variable. There was a tea break half-way through the session, when mothers were encouraged to go upstairs for tea, leaving the babies in the care of the two group leaders. I arrived thirty minutes after the start of the two-hour session and spent one hour observing.

I focus on six of the children, describing the patterns I perceived over several weeks. I describe how each of them used the time and space provided, what they paid attention to, and how they interacted with the people and objects in the room—how they decide what is "good" in the world. I was interested in both the mothers' relationships with, and influence on, their children, and the babies' use of, and influence on, their mothers. I will make speculations about psychological and emotional states expressed through the babies' play and the defences that seemed embedded in some of the babies' activity and/or passivity. The language of movement is, of course, one of the central modes of both expression and perception for infants. Movement is the *first* mode of perception, as the vestibular nerves that govern the registering of movement are the first to develop in utero. Movement, therefore, plays an important role in "establishing the baseline" for other perceptual processes (Cohen, 1987).

### Sherry—psychically twinned with mother

Against this background, I shall begin with a baby called Sherry, whom I first observed when she was eight months old.

> Mum was on the floor, holding Sherry on her lap, facing outwards. They looked very much alike, both with round faces, short black hair, and weighty, rounded bodies. Sherry seemed very alert to the space, however, while mother did not. Sherry brought toys to her mouth: the tip of a Telly Tubby's headgear, a plastic box handle. As mum held her facing out, sitting on mum's knee, Sherry seemed to be very active in her extremities, especially kicking her feet and mobilizing her legs. Mum turned her so they faced each other, and held her under her armpits so that her feet just touched the ground. She then lifted her up and cradled her in her arms as if she were a younger baby. Sherry seemed to struggle against this, making some sounds. Mum said, "Are you tired?"
>
> I felt uncomfortable, and wondered why mum seemed to want to keep hold of Sherry. Sherry then pressed her feet strongly against mum's

thigh, sending energy right through her own body. This seemed to give her a firm contact with mum, as well as exerting her ability and desire to use her weight. Her intention seemed to be to move. Mother continued to cradle Sherry on her lap.

This sequence was frustrating to watch; there was a conflict of interests between mother and daughter that I sensed in my own body. Sherry wanted to expand her horizons, but mother seemed to need Sherry to remain a passive infant baby.

Sherry seemed motivated not just by the sensuality of physical objects but also by her curiosity to explore the surrounding space. In movement terms, we could say she was exploring the element of weight (physical sensation), but was also motivated by the more mentally affined element of space. Mother was intent on using her weight to keep Sherry close, adhesively stuck, skin to skin. Perhaps mother's own infantile needs were being touched upon. Projective identification, the unconscious transmission of "psychobiological states" (Schore, 2002), did not seem to be working in Sherry's favour here.

A similar sequence was recorded the following week. Mother sat behind Sherry on the floor:

When Sherry reached forward as if to explore a toy, which would have taken her on to her belly, mum caught her round the hips and lightly, almost unconsciously, restrained her. Sherry didn't seem phased by this. Sherry and mum remained sitting for quite some time, Sherry mouthing the yellow wooden block, mum occasionally stroking Sherry's hair.

Mum again seems to resist her daughter's impulse towards mobility, towards entering into a "transitional space" where she could begin to find symbolic substitutes for mother and the breast. Instead, they are both lulled into an internally focused, sensuous, dream state merging (weight and flow). One wonders what has happened to Sherry's more active impulses towards separation. It would appear that she has been able to split them off and perhaps use them against herself to blot out her own aggressive feelings. There is an aura of dissociation and depression surrounding them both. Hinshelwood suggests that, "Depression seems to be a process of mourning which has gone wrong because of the special strength of hatred toward the object" (1994, p. 19).

Two weeks later I wrote:

> Sherry appeared to have grown, as if inflated since two weeks ago. It
> was disturbing to see, as she looked fat and seemed less mobile because
> of it. She sat on the floor with mother right behind. Sherry would reach
> out only as far as her arm would extend to select a toy. She would
> always put the toy in her mouth immediately.

By this observation Sherry seemed to have become quite
compliant and passive, joining mother in a mutually deadening
adhesive bond. I noted: *Her active use of weight to reach and/or push
was almost gone.* In reaching for toys, Sherry's external world
seemed to have adjusted to fit the size of mother's lap, and one suspects there was not a very robust internal object to enliven her internal world either. She seems to have become a rather lifeless little
girl, latching on to easily accessible objects as if latching on to an
ever-ready breast, exploring them only with her mouth. Objects
were not used symbolically, but as symbolic equivalents of the
breast. Any wish to explore a different way of being in the world
seems to have been forsaken.

In movement terms, Sherry and mother share a dull, passive
experience of weight and a neutralized experience of flow. There is
no sense of active weight or sensuous physicality. A lively sense of
being in space and time is seen to be discouraged and therefore not
assimilated into Sherry's repertoire. This was also exemplified
when mother went to tea. On one occasion, after mum left:

> Sherry began to twist her body and lean forward towards a baby near
> her. The group leader said "Oh, you're going to crawl!" Sherry looked
> at me and at the leader, and didn't follow through to move forward,
> but sat back down and stayed very still. Moments later, Sherry had to
> be carried out to mum as she had begun to cry inconsolably.

I wondered if she thought of mum at the moment she was about to
crawl away, but found she could not challenge mother's unconscious pressure to remain passive.

On another occasion,

> mother placed Sherry in front of the mirror before leaving the room.
> Sherry held a blanket to her mouth and looked at herself in the mirror.

She also watched things going on behind her in the mirror. She seemed content like this for quite a while.

Here we can see what might be a preference for a flat surface view of the world, a two-dimensional view, rather than having a sense of actually being present in a three-dimensional space. It was as if she had not been weaned on to the liveliness of the outside world from the adhesive surface identification with mum, rather than a projective identification that could be received by her mother.

The contrast between the flat reflection and being present in a three-dimensional space was illustrated again at ten months and three weeks:

Sherry held on to the elastic band which supported the books, just behind her mum. She pulled herself up to stand. She handled a book briefly Then she sat down, behind and to the side of mother, facing away from the books and into the room, staring at all the activity with a wary expression on her face. Her body conveyed a posture of fear or paranoia, it seemed to me, as she sat leaning into the wall, head pulled down and forward and twisted to an angle, body also hunched to the side. As if she were hoping she was invisible. She picked up a piece of paper and began to chew the edge of it.

Sherry can tolerate the mirror view, but when she finds herself facing the real world, she appears to feel lost and filled with persecutory phantasies. It seemed that Sherry had given up her early curiosity about the world in order to sustain a delusion of closeness with mother. It seems that, although mother tries her best to offer her idea of "containment" to her daughter, containment is not what Sherry needs at this stage. She needs encouragement to use her energy and to mobilize herself to enter the outside world. In phantasy, one suspects she feels her mobility would be dangerous not only for herself but for her mother.

In movement terms, the elements of time and space, together comprising Laban's "awake state" and an object-related alertness, are the ones that would support Sherry in moving on. Time and weight or weight and space, the components of the "near state", and the "stable state", respectively, could also be important, the former in order to develop her sense of agency by becoming physically decisive and self-motivated, the latter to help her in simply feeling present in a three-dimensional world.

In several observations, I saw Sherry move into what seemed like a rather un-babylike physical position, which appeared to be a compromise between remaining inert and making a tentative effort toward exploration:

> She lowered her torso, twisting to the side until she was lying supported on an elbow, resting her head in her hand. From here she could bring a ball to her mouth with her free right hand. The ball was larger than could fit so she opened her mouth wide and put the ball to touch her open mouth.

I felt that this position was an expression of Sherry's ambivalent and anxious feelings about separation. It represented a rather clever solution that did not create unbearable anxiety. From the position she had adopted she had the advantage of being able to keep an eye on mother as well as see the rest of the room. On the rare occasions when Sherry did, in later sessions, begin to crawl, her movement was terribly stiff, seeming to convey the same complex conflict of interests. I felt her harsh superego had taken up residence in her stiff neck.

> Sherry crawled to the ball pond where other children were gathering and clambering in. She placed her hands on the pond structure and looked back at mum, smiling. She repeated her look to mum several times; her attention seemed absorbed with having mother's eye on her, and not at all with the other children or the pond. She crawled back to mum. I noticed her crawl was very stiff. She held her head and neck in a fixed, slightly twisted position that affected her freedom of movement. As she neared mum Sherry began to cry, as if she did not want to have to go the rest of the way unaided. Mum picked her up, sat her on her lap and handed her the cup of juice.

In movement terms, such locomotion might normally involve an activation of weight and a sense of time in its progression. But here, the outstanding features were the opposite: bound flow, as if flow had replaced her capacity to really use her weight; and her latching on to mum with her eyes throughout once again reflects her mental preoccupation (space). For Sherry, this represented not a perception of the real space, but a confused mixture of the internal world and the outer one

This is an example of where, as an observer, I could identify with Sherry's psychophysical state. I could sense her predicament in my body, my neck and shoulders especially. I felt her tension and her adhesion to mother.

*Perhaps the reader can also take a moment to sense this baby's state in your own body.*

It is my feeling that LMA provides needed categories that help us sharpen our embodied attentiveness, which might otherwise be simply registered as anxiety or conflict. McDougall writes "When there is little potential psychic 'space' between mother and child, then the growing child . . . may have difficulty organizing its own psychic reality and performing caretaking functions for herself" (McDougall, 1989, p. 71). One hopes that, given time, Sherry may find both the stimulation from the outside world and the inner creative spark to fire her towards mobility and interest in the world; and that her mother will be able to recognize the value for both of them in becoming separate, so as not to impede Sherry's or her own development.

## Rodney—get me out of here

A very different character from Sherry, Rodney could hardly bear to modulate his frantic, constant movement through space. Rodney seemed driven on a random, yet urgent exploration. I felt he was searching, without knowing what he was searching for; and his desire to move exceeded his ability to make the physical adjustments required. It was as if his wish for mobility was not grounded in the recognition of having a body to mobilize. I will try to illustrate. I first saw Rodney when he was seven months old. He had not yet figured out how to move through space.

He was trying to crawl into the space toward the toys. He showed a great effort and exertion of will. He used his feet to press the floor behind him. This lifted his knees from the ground. He did not really support himself with his hands either. He reached forward with his hands as he pushed, and flopped on to his belly. But now that his upper body was heavily on the ground, the effort to move forward was an impossibly frustrating task. Mum comments that he was frustrated even as a very little baby.

This pattern was often repeated. Sometimes Rodney would put his fingers into his mouth after a jolt like this. Rodney could not mobilize his weight to support his intention to go forward. It is interesting to note that in Laban's analysis the sagittal dimension and plane (the "wheel plane" that moves forward and back) has an affinity with the element of time and lacks a relationship to the horizontal dimension and its affinity with the reflective element of space. The sense of urgency seemed paramount in Rodney's drive to advance through space.

He often followed his frustrated attempts at mobility by putting the nearest toy in his mouth. By doing so, he recovered some sensory experience of himself (weight) as well as giving in to an earlier, perhaps more appropriate, stage of infancy, that of being safely held and dependent on a good object. He rather seemed to deny mother's value by his drive to get away.

At 10½ months, Rodney had mastered crawling. I noted:

> He spent most of the hour moving round the room from object to object, never spending more than a few seconds with anything. Pushing with his feet, he seemed to dive into the floor with his head, as he moved among the toys.

In Laban terms, although he was keen to be let loose in the space, time and flow seemed to be the primary motivating factors. There was both a lack of physical weight, which is linked with having an intention to *do* something, and a lack of any mindful attention to space. He seemed to be propelled by an inner urgency and agitation rather than a sense of curiosity. A clue to a source of his anxiety may have been revealed in the following, at eleven months:

> He pulled himself up to stand at the table where he placed the block and batted at a book. Mum said when she tries to read to him on her lap, he pulls to get down and away. Mum then described how she had had a terrible accident herself as a baby. She climbed on to a table to look out the window and fell, cracking her skull. She had a bad concussion and was lucky to have survived.

The sharing by mother of her own terrible trauma during infancy seemed to provide a possible explanation for Rodney's own anxiety. Mother, too, had little sense of having been contained and could only provide an anxious container for her baby. At worst, the normal process of projective identification was reversed. Rodney was needed to contain mother's projections and was understandably overwhelmed. This provides a possible explanation for his fleeing through space in a meaningless way, with nothing to hold onto. In the following sequence, at eleven months, mother plays a game of putting Rodney in a precarious situation that both thrilled and agitated him, a kind of controlled re-enactment of her own infantile trauma, making the hypothesis of Rodney introjecting an anxious object all the more graphic and the protective function of his omnipotent striving more understandable.

> Mum played a game in which she threw Rodney on his back on to a cushion. I thought this seemed slightly odd, to drop him and toss him like that. He smiled and she repeated it four times. I sensed a bit of unease in other mothers.

Later in the same session:

> When mum returned from tea, she lifted Rodney from behind, under the armpits, and sat him on her lap, only then turning him to face her. He seemed discombobulated at first, but then he gave a faint smile of recognition before he pulled to get down.

Here we see mother's contributing to Rodney's disorientation and manic behaviour by taking him by surprise, only later letting him know she was available for a face-to-face meeting. He received a sudden startle. This can be thought of as mainly representing suddenness and free flow in LMA. Mother and baby seemed to share the state of mind produced by the mobile state.

There was finally a change in this pattern for Rodney and mum when he was having much discomfort teething. Mum and baby were exhausted from a sleepless night and I thought they both appeared a little depressed. I wrote:

> Rodney stayed nearby mum. Mum rubbed stuff on his gums with her finger. Later he was able to go exploring, but not in such a manic way as before.

The depression that the couple seemed to feel allowed the manic, time-driven aspect of their mood to give way to a more thoughtful and sensual presence. They seemed to have stopped rushing and allowed themselves to stay put, to be present in suffering the painful feelings that were around. The result seemed to be something more like the emotionally based spell drive, an intense "timeless" moment, incorporating the three elements of weight, flow, and space. Rodney's moving away had a more three-dimensional quality than before implying real separation and in Kleinian terms, an experience of the depressive position.

Both Rodney and Sherry shared similar movement qualities with their mothers, as if they had taken these on through adhesive-like identification with their primary objects. In both cases, themes that were evident in the mothers were also evident in their babies. The babies' primitive defences, or second skin protections, reflected something of those shared qualities. In the first couple, the tendency was to freeze up deep down (under a cushion of plumpness) in order to deal with difficult feelings. In the second pair, the tendency was to rush or take flight.

### Sara—a measured approach

Unlike the first two couples, Sara had strikingly different movement qualities and temperament from her mother; yet, because this mother seemed mostly well attuned to her daughter's needs, Sara was more able to express herself and explore her world in her own way, at her own pace. I was immediately struck by the way this little girl exuded a sense of presence in body, in time, and in space. She was already thirteen months old when I first saw her. She had been walking for just two weeks. I wrote:

> She was tall, red-haired, and very appealing. She was very measured in her movement, using a combination of direct focus, sustainment in time and light weight. [This combination, in Laban's terms, creates the Effort action of "glide".] She used her hands to delicately touch the space, with a lack of tension, and a very considered, and thoughtful presence. Mother had a much quicker tempo; she seemed to have to hold back her utter excitement and adoration for Sara. Clearly able to

take in the overview of the space as well, she initiated conversation with other mothers and made observations about their babies. After a while, she gave Sara a breastfeed for a minute or two, which seemed to suit them both.

Whereas Sara's two predominant movement qualities were weight and space, the components of Laban's "stable state", her mother's seemed much more based in time and space, the "awake state". Mother seemed to admire her daughter's physical stability in the space, and Sara seemed to acknowledge the keenly watchful eye of mother. They came together easily for a brief feed, which, characterized primarily by sensory and emotional experience, was a recuperation for both in the "dream state"; and then Sara confidently moved away again. She seemed to have internalized a good object that helped her to feel quite sturdy in the world. Sara's clarity contrasted with the other two babies, who seemed to be more motivated by unconscious phantasies having to do with enmeshment with mother. Sara seemed able to give her full attention to the real world as she took it in from moment to moment.

At 13½ months,

Sara held Mother's index finger as they entered the room, later than the others. Mum said to her, "Look at all the babies." Sara walked a step forward, still holding mum's finger, so her arm was extended backwards. Mum waited for Sara to let go. They stood together like this for some time, Sara facing the room and Mum standing behind. Sara watched, very serious as she stood. She seemed thoughtful as she released mother's hand. Each movement that followed was calm and measured, a bend of the knees, a step, her hand supporting on the space.

I was struck by the way this couple had an ability to inhabit their own separate time and space, which allowed a meaningful non-verbal dialogue to take place. Mother could adapt her normally quick tempo, allowing Sara the time she needed to let go. Mother did not in any way impinge upon her daughter's freedom to explore, yet she provided her with a sense of being safely contained.

Three weeks later, the pair were seen to be allowing further development to take place.

Sara walked to the table beside me. She pulled out the small chair; I helped with this and she tried to climb into the chair. At first she stood on the chair, then slowly bent her knees to squat. Mum came and said, "That's right, sit 'til you can feel the chair," which Sara did. She sat, swinging her legs, and mum sighed with pride. She said, "Look at her swinging her legs . . . she's not a baby any more."

In this sequence mum again seemed to be rejoicing in her daughter's developing ability, treasuring every moment; while at the same time her sigh conveyed a sadness in acknowledging the passing of time. Mum's lively tempo had slowed down in this moment of sighing; her primary movement qualities had become space and flow (thoughts and feelings). Sara's qualities were time and weight, as she embodies a rhythmic sense of agency. They were in opposite states of "remote" and "near". They did not seem to be enmeshed in an unconscious merging. The only constraint I perceived in Sara's movement and play was a sense that the element of flow, which might motivate a more emotional involvement with the world, was very much in the background. This gave Sara a cool, calculated, and rational approach to the world, which may have been her way of keeping less manageable feelings about weaning at bay.

## Alice—faulty skin container

Alice was one year old when I met her, and she stood out from the others as she seemed so frail—a tiny, pale, blonde waif. I wondered if her mother had mild learning difficulties, as it was very hard for her to keep her attention on Alice or even to stay in the room. Alice had a chronic eczema-like skin condition and had to have her forearms wrapped in bandages so as not to scratch herself.

Rather than being able to feel protected by a mother who contained her and whom she could introject, Alice's skin seemed to declare her frustrating irritation at the lack of containment. Her bandaging and her skin condition seemed a prototypical example of Bick's second skin formations. "Until the containing functions have been introjected, the concept of a space within the self cannot arise" (Bick, 1968).

Alice's skin condition may have represented an unconscious attempt to create a protective boundary for herself. By scratching, she could feel the "me–not me" boundary all the more. This way of attacking herself put her in the position of being both the aggressor and the victim. Alice's condition portrayed a fraught and complicated picture of the mother–daughter relationship, in which, to use Bion's language (1962), there was no space to make thoughts thinkable.

In the following excerpts, I will describe the way in which Alice and mother seemed to co-exist in separate spaces, unable to take each other in. This seemed to suggest the kind of social and communication difficulties associated with autistic disorders (Alvarez & Reid, 1999). I will also describe the peculiar way Alice had of locomoting through space, in which an inner struggle seemed to be played out.

These excerpts take place when Alice was between thirteen and seventeen months old:

> Alice's mum sat in a chair next to me. Alice sat on the floor with her wrist mitts on. She had scratches all over her face. When she looked at her mum, it was with a wary sideways glance. They did not really make eye contact. Alice travelled across the space by using her right leg, stretched out in front and pulling herself with it. Her left leg was folded backward at the knee. She sat and looked round including towards the ceiling, then used her right leg to turn herself round a complete circle, surveying the room. Alice smiled as she explored, giving me the feeling she had an imaginary life.

Alice's looking round seemed to be an other-worldly kind of seeing, not really taking in the space she inhabited or the people. Her impish smile was appealing, but it seemed dissociated from here and now reality. I thought it was evidence of another kind of second skin formation, that of wrapping herself in an imaginary world (Jackson & Nowers, 2002).

> . . . she dragged herself forward with her outstretched right leg. It was as though the right half of her wanted to go and the left was frozen.

The body-half split in Alice's movement seemed to describe a part of her that was eager to explore the world; but the other side, perhaps in an attempt to stand for the missing maternal containment, was just as determined to hold Alice firmly in place. In movement terms, the split can be described as being between an "awake state" half—motivated by time and space, wishing to explore the outside world (albeit in a possibly hallucinatory way)—and its opposite, "dream state", expressed with light weight and bound flow, the inner focused state, motivating the inward folding left half. Perhaps it is a hopeful sign, considering the impoverishment of her internal world, that the urge to be "awake" wins out and that she manages to move at all.

*If the reader takes a moment to sense your own body, perhaps the extreme inner conflict represented in a body-half split like Alice's, in which one half is interned and the other is outward reaching, can be felt.*

... she pulled herself to stand holding a chair. It took great effort, which seemed to have to do with both weakness and poor ability to organize her movement. She stood with feet turned right out to the sides, and her weight seemed to be on the insides of her feet. She did not seem well supported at all; it was largely her arms on the table that supported her weight. This was painful to watch. She turned to look at her mother, who had left the room shortly before. She lowered herself to the floor, sat, looked toward mother's empty spot, and then to me. ... When mum returned, she picked Alice up and sat her on her lap. They both looked past each other without focusing on each other.

Despite Alice's best efforts to hold herself, she showed a lack of support particularly in her effort to stand. A sense of an internal space or an internalized good object seemed almost non-existent. This was depicted again:

She sat on the floor. It was not clear why, but she tipped backwards, hitting her head against a corner of the wall.

Again we can see the effect of a lack of supportive maternal backing for Alice. The falling over backwards implies a lack of support for the spine, which Haag states is the "most important contact surface" as it "fits closely against the curves of the uterine cavity" (Haag, 1991). Haag gives equal importance to the soles of the feet, and here, again, we have seen that Alice is on shaky ground.

In the following excerpt we see that both mother and Alice avoid contact, preferring to turn to others instead. It was difficult for both parties to recognize and accept their primary relationship with each other.

Alice's mum opened the door for me when I arrived at the building and she continued to leave the playroom each time she saw through the window that someone was approaching or heard the buzzer. She opened the door and carried in babies while their mothers locked the prams. She said she liked her job, that she was bringing in babies off the street. Alice sat on the floor near me. She seemed to be aware of these impulsive exits mum made and her return with other babies, though she did not seem to watch this directly.

And—

When mum returned from tea, Alice smiled, but turned and reached for the worker. The worker did not respond and instead pointed saying, "Look! There's mummy!" Alice looked in mum's general direction and smiled distractedly. Mum smiled back as she knelt near her and put her face near to Alice's. Mum seemed, at this moment, to be very adoring. However, it seemed that the moments of contact were brief, and when they did happen, one or other interrupted the connection and returned to the pervasive pattern, as if real embodied contact was nearly impossible. Mutual awareness in space and time (the "awake state"), was briefly possible, but sustaining it seemed too much to bear.

I felt that mother's primary movement qualities were time and flow. Even though she was ostensibly responding to real external events, the actions of jumping up and exiting the room seemed motivated less by thinking (space) or the impulse to do any physical action (weight) than by the need to respond to an urgent unconscious emotional urge (free flow). This predominance of time and flow characterizes Laban's "mobile state". Alice, on the other hand, seemed to be motivated by a predominance of space and flow in her seemingly imaginary world. These elements characterize Laban's "remote state".

I had the feeling that Alice received lots of attention from the group leaders, as did her mother, and that this, as well as the proximity of other lively babies and mums had a positive and stimulating effect on this very needy couple. This description of Alice provides an example of the way in which the added perspective of LMA in infant observation could help enormously in thinking both about the patterns Alice used to achieve a kind of equilibrium, and the encouragement of patterns that might support her growth.

## The emergence of patterns

In each of the four babies presented so far, we can observe repeated patterns in their activity and behaviour. With the probable exception of Sara, the patterns seem to suggest that there were so-called second skin formations, or pseudo-independent structures, present. In Kleinian terms, only Sara appeared to have achieved the predominantly three-dimensional perspective associated with the depressive position, the ability to relate to mother as a whole, multi-faceted object. In the other cases, the relationships were predominantly two-dimensional relationships to part objects, characterized by the splitting and unconscious phantasy associated with the developmentally earlier paranoid–schizoid position.

Fraiberg (1982) described three categories of pathological defences in infancy. She speculated that the use of *avoidance, freezing*, and *fighting* are derived from the primitive biological instincts for fight or flight. I think we see the tendency toward each one of these defences respectively in the three babies: Sherry's protection was her tendency to freeze, Rodney's was to take flight, and Alice's protection was to avoid contact. Avoidant or inconsistent behaviour in the mother has been shown to produce avoidant attachment in the baby (Ainsworth, Blehar, Waters, & Wall, 1978; Fraiberg, 1982).

As it happened, each of these three babies shared similar configurations of movement preferences and similar states of mind with their mothers. This does pose the question: in what ways do the mothers' themes get reflected in the infants' activity (Salo et al., 1997)? Sara and her mother had different movement profiles and they seemed to have the most conscious and clear relationship of the four.

It would be an oversimplification to suggest, however, that there is a direct correlation between shared movement qualities and a tendency toward enmeshment or part object relating. The next mother–infant dyad I describe shared predominant traits, but did not give any evidence of being enmeshed in an adhesive-type relationship.

### Amy—liveliness and its effect on others

Amy only started attending the group in the last couple of months I was observing. She was just six months old, but she was already exploring crawling. She stands out in my memory vividly because she was so spontaneous in her embodied exploration of the external world. The keen alertness in her eyes seemed to inspire the natural but precocious development of her movement from crawling to standing at ten months.

> When she caught my eye, I felt my own eyes widen in response and a feeling of wonder came over me. Her mother had the same curiosity and initiative. Her mother said Amy has no fear.

She was graceful and poised in her movement, reflecting what seemed like a supreme confidence. I felt this had something to do with the fact that her mother, more than any of the other mothers, entered into the space with her in a playful, creative way. She would lie down or crawl, following Amy's lead, exploring the toys with her daughter. She told me that she herself had walked when she was ten months old. In movement terms, I saw a balanced use of all the movement qualities in both mother and daughter. This sense of integration and presence on all levels at once—physical, mental, and emotional—gave an intensity and vividness to Amy's movement. At seven months, however, Amy was not yet sturdy enough to sustain this confidence in mother's absence.

> . . . Amy smiled broadly when her (or another's) mum had her attention. Her feet seemed as active and integrated as her hands as she sat. She was drawn to crawl towards a toy. Her crawl was smooth and appeared effortless. At teatime, Amy's mum was the last to leave; she stood at the door. Amy lost her balance for a moment and began to topple over backwards; she was assisted by a worker. Amy did manage to engage with a toy that had a mirror and played a tune, but soon began to look round and cry. She seemed very distressed and was carried to mum. When they returned, Amy seemed vulnerable. Mum held her quietly.

Without mother's loving presence and particularly her eyes on Amy, she lost contact with the internal support she felt when mum was present. She was able to keep an eye on herself for a moment using the mirror, but this capacity to contain herself had not been built up strongly enough yet. Mother seemed well attuned to Amy's need for both room to explore the big wide world, and a feeling of safety and containment.

In terms of movement qualities, I felt that although time and space, the "awake state" may have represented the primary state of mind of this couple, the sense of physical and emotional embodiment (weight and flow) was also integral to their activity; I felt all four basic Effort elements were active. This intensity of involvement and enthusiasm gave me a feeling of energy and excitement just to witness them. It struck me that Amy unwittingly attracted the attention of other babies as well. They would often reach out to touch her as she passed them, and she showed great fascination for them too.

How was it that their clarity of presence, both individually and in relationship, seemed to actually wake up the others and enliven the space? I suggest that because they were firing on all cylinders, so to speak, all senses open and active, the others were unconsciously impelled to align themselves with their openness, as if they were given permission to take in something of the goodness and life of this couple as nourishment for their own internal worlds. The flip side of this, of course, are the envious feelings that may also have been stirred up. This kind of transmission and absorption of feeling states through non-verbal communication is central to transference and countertransference processes.

### Oscar—dealing with an impending rival

Last, there was Oscar, a very sociable and good-natured baby. What was particularly interesting when observing him over time were the ways in which his play and moods altered as it gradually became apparent that his mother was due to have another baby who would be born when Oscar was sixteen months old. Oscar seemed to use the playgroup to work through his feelings about the momentous impending change in his world.

The first time I saw him, at nine months:

Oscar sat within reach of Rodney. He crawled to Rodney, reaching for his face, wanting to lightly touch him and mouth him. Though his mum gently restrained him, he repeated the attempt to make contact over and over.

Oscar's ease with making contact, his openness to others, made him quite appealing. His natural curiosity and relaxed attitude gave a sense of someone in possession of his own mind, not preoccupied with many conflicting feelings. He shared this ease with his mother, who could easily empathize with and adore Oscar. They both seemed to be able to use energy efficiently and productively. This contrasted with the anxious over-enthusiasm of Rodney and his mother described earlier, who both seemed to expend a great deal more energy and not really get anywhere.

Three weeks later:

Mother left for tea. Crawling, Oscar sped toward the ball pond, and he clambered in. After some time swishing his legs about, he climbed out. He seemed on the one hand to be exploring happily, but he also seemed to be pushing himself to stand and stay up. He looked for reas-surance to adults, smiling a fake smile as he made eye contact. He picked up a book in each hand and toddled with them. Then Oscar sat down in the middle of the room, and suddenly began to cry. I noted to myself that this is a very different Oscar.

Oscar seemed to instinctively head for the sensual inside space of the ball pond where he could be totally supported when mother left, as if immediately finding an alternative support system. He followed this by a premature show of strength in his attempt to walk tall, with the hope of attracting admiration; but this ended in collapse and despair. When mum returned,

she sat holding him on her lap facing out. She put her hand on his back, reaching under his overalls to touch his shirt. They both leant forward as if feeling sad.

With hindsight, I felt the fact of an impending "intruder" was clearly present.

Initially, Oscar's primary movement qualities seemed to be a flexible attitude towards space and a sustained attitude towards time (a particular variation of the "awake state"), in his openness to exploring his links with others. These were combined with his use of light weight to perform various actions. His movement seemed efficient and appropriate to accomplish what he wanted. But, in the later description, the emotional element of flow began to motivate, sometimes a reckless free flow, other times a bound flow constriction of energy. This is combined with a narrowing of focus and a pressure to increase his tempo. His attempt to assert strong weight in his walking was eclipsed by the binding of flow. These changes characterized his growing insecurity and the resulting attempts to maintain control.

> When Oscar was thirteen months old, mother was obviously pregnant. I noted upon arriving, Oscar reached for the ark toy. He opened the roof and reached in. He took out the elephant and threw it.

This strong, sudden, direct action of a punch as Oscar selects and gets rid of the largest beast seemed to leave no doubt about his feelings towards mother. (Or perhaps the elephant symbolized a combined parental object, combining the male trunk with the large belly.) His mother gave every indication of being able to receive and tolerate his angry projection.

> Oscar then stood and began to toddle across the room to where a three-month-old baby was lying in its carrycot. He seemed to be gentle as he knelt by the baby and watched it. Then he stood, looking forlornly into the room.

After some initial interest, he seemed defeated by the idea of having to share his life with a tiny baby, as well as being forced to give up his own occupancy of the baby space prematurely.

He appeared to be working hard through symbolic play to understand his situation right up until he left the group at fourteen months when the family moved. In living through a grieving process together, mother and Oscar were able to take the good with the bad, so to speak, about the new baby. However difficult, feelings were allowed to flow and be explored. The balance of movement qualities was not unduly distorted by a second skin adaptation to defend against reality. The resilient bond already established between mother and Oscar supported them in working through difficult feelings.

## Summary

Through describing the foregoing material from an observational study of several babies within a group setting, and in the process, weaving together LMA and psychoanalytic thinking, I hope to have given the reader some understanding of the potential that each perspective offers the other. Psychoanalytic thinking helps to elucidate hypotheses about the babies' internal worlds and primary relationships; and the movement vocabulary helps to recognize the specific ways in which their psychic states are embodied or defended against. The movement view may help observers to gain a *felt sense* of these sensoriaffective states that do not necessarily depend on words, by attending to their own bodies.

It does seem possible in each case to describe primitive defences in terms of an imbalance in movement qualities, some of which are overly dominant while others appear absent. I suggest that the body registers, reflects, and responds to the psychic experience. I am trying, therefore, to show how movement can provide an added dimension of insight by making the sensoriaffective experience more explicit, and making psychoanalytic metaphors like "second skin" more clearly defined and measurable. It is hoped that the reader will have been able to identify with the embodied experience of the various mothers and babies.

I am suggesting that what an infant observer may have "picked up" intuitively may be given further definition when given *embodied attentiveness*; intuitive responses are usually to something nonverbal. One notices that something is out of balance. Sherry's inhibition in the use of space and time (awake state), or Rodney's weakness in the stability gained by weight and space (stable state) are examples of how LMA makes the intuitive response more decipherable.

Being able to see from this perspective may offer other options when thinking about how to provide the conditions for growth and change in a therapy setting. Equally important is that psychoanalysis provides a theoretical framework within which movement therapists' observations of patterns and preferences can be given added meaning and context.

# CHAPTER SEVEN

# Falling into space

"I'm falling down. Help me with the meaning of it all"

(Seen on a Samuel Beckett website)

Melanie Klein developed the field of child psychotherapy around the premise that play is the child's "most important medium of expression", and that by its nature, play "puts action in place of words" (Klein, 1932). In this chapter, I illustrate the way in which a child's expressive movement powerfully communicated significant themes and patterns that reflected her unconscious phantasies.

I visited Anny, a 3–4-year-old girl weekly for one year as part of the "Young Child Observation" module of the Psychoanalytic Observational Studies course at the Tavistock Clinic. In returning two years later to the detailed notes made after each observation, in preparation for writing this chapter, I was struck by the fact that although Anny's play was thought about with great care, and many insights were gleaned from the material in the seminar group, there were significant themes and patterns of a *physical* nature that I noticed in the re-reading which had not been noted previously either by myself, despite my training as a movement analyst, or by my group.

It seemed that my later intention to go through the material with the aim of integrating the perspectives of movement analysis and psychoanalysis, may have made it possible to bring out these new themes, thus adding to or underpinning the layers of meaning already derived. I wondered whether, with a child like Anny, who made such good use of language in her highly symbolic play, the non-verbal expression and communication may have been less prominent to the observing eye and mind; and whether themes of a non-verbal nature may have been lying behind the language, so to speak. With this thought in mind I will present some material which illustrates the main theme that crystallized in the rereading—that of falling.

## Background

Anny was the elder of two girls in what might be called an ordinary middle-class family. Her father was North American and her mother was English. Father was mostly absent from the scene as he worked long hours and his work often entailed travel. Mother had given up her career as a teacher when Anny was born, and since then she "enjoyed being a full-time mum". Anny's anxieties about rival babies, and her Oedipal feelings of aggression and guilt were, on the one hand, typical of a child her age. But what was different for Anny and for all the family was that, as I gradually came to know, mother had suffered her first miscarriage between Anny and her ten-month-old sister, Cora; and there were two more miscarriages during the year I observed the family. The first of these was two and a half months after starting, and just after the Christmas break. In retrospect I realized that during that year, mother was probably either preoccupied with being pregnant or with having lost a pregnancy. Because of the series of losses she had sustained in a short period, the seminar group felt there was undoubtedly a painful accumulation of unresolved grief in mother, and also a heightened sense of anxiety in Anny. In taking a fresh look at this material, it seems that falling down may well describe exactly the kinds of unconscious fears and anxieties Anny felt confronted with during this period coloured by enormous losses.

## Initial meeting with mother

My initial meeting was with mother alone, for the purpose of making arrangements for the regular weekly observations. On that occasion she spoke of Anny as "self contained", saying, "She's just like I was when I was little." There was an atmosphere of calm and orderliness at this meeting that I wrote in my notes felt strangely stifling. Mother sat quite still, hands neatly folded in her lap as we spoke. In retrospect, it seemed very much a picture of someone who wanted to keep things in place by holding still.

Thinking in movement terms, the predominant qualities I felt present in mother at this meeting—after absorbing her state, and later translating my experience into Laban terms—were (bound) flow and (flexible) space. Flow is the element associated with feelings; space is associated with thinking. The two together make up the "remote state", in which thoughts and feelings predominate. This particular combination of flow and space—bound and flexible—depicts an aspect of the "remote state" that may describe someone trying to keep things under control when there are many thoughts and feelings to cope with at once, which may otherwise threaten to overwhelm. On occasion I felt flow was replaced by a greater physical presence (light weight), giving her more of a sense of stability and concentration.

But, generally speaking, the motivating factors of *weight*—which would have bolstered a sense of embodiment and vitality—or a relationship, internally or externally, with the decisiveness associated with the element of *time* were less apparent. With hindsight, I wondered whether these elements posed a threat of loss, as if too much spontaneity or engagement with the body were felt to be dangerous.

> Perhaps the reader can take a moment to try to embody this timeless, weightless state, by attending to their own flow of feelings and awareness of space, the qualities which define the remote state.

## Identification with mother

When I met Anny, I noted that indeed there was a part of her character that seemed to be something like her mother or what I suspected mother meant when she said that Anny was "self-contained". Particularly in the early sessions, Anny liked to take charge in an adult way. When in this "adult" mode, she was meticulous in her attention to detail, and precise placement of objects in space. Her focus was, using Laban's term, extremely direct, pinpointedly narrow. I thought that this way of relating to space was sometimes exaggerated and at these times incorporated bound flow. This rather cramped attitude seemed to sometimes serve the purpose of keeping out any acknowledgement of her sister's presence. Anny strove to keep Cora out of sight, and thus, out of mind.

Anny's identification with mother was a recurring feature of her behaviour, which seemed to give her a sense of control, and lessen her feelings of dependence, anxiety and indeed, at times, of falling apart. Rather than mirroring mother's "remote state", however, I felt that Anny's identification with mother could be characterized by her use of efficient, productive actions. In Laban terms these would be action drive elements such as pressing, dabbing, or gliding—all of which are motivated by weight, space, and time, all featuring direct rather than flexible focus in space. The identification with adults and their "grown-up behaviour" seemed to be one form of defence Anny used to keep difficult feelings at bay.

Flow, bound or free, seemed to become predominant when the sense of identification with mother could no longer be sustained. As the observations progressed, Anny came to make use of me as someone with whom she could explore more uncontrolled feelings and dangerous thoughts and impulses, in which flow became a predominant feature. The alternating rhythm between identification with mother and rebelling against this, often with wild flowing action and heightened passions (which could sometimes represent another kind of defence of a manic nature), followed by a return to "adult" control, provided an interesting theme in itself.

## The theme of falling

I sensed that the theme of falling may have been the essential image to describe Anny's concerns about mother's miscarriages and the phantasies about their effect on her (and her effect on them). Anny had many actual falls during the observations. She also talked about falls that had happened outside observation time; and fear of the life-threatening dangers of falling was expressed by both Anny and mother. Variations on the theme, in movements of sliding off of or flopping down on to furniture, as well as play that involved dolls either falling or being thrown down, also stood out. I do not know why this theme, which now seems apparent, did not register in the first instance. I can only surmise that when words are present they tend to take precedence when considering what is meaningful.

On the whole, falling seemed to represent quite the opposite of the kind of identification with mother described previously. The need for such identification—the sense of focus, practicality and control—may have served to give Anny a feeling of containment. It is impossible not to speculate on the parallels and similarities between the experience of falling—in which solid ground shifts, disappears, or can no longer be trusted, in which there may be a feeling of being dropped, left hanging in mid-air, or allowed to slip away into a void—and the shocking loss provoked by miscarriage. Melanie Klein (1946) used the metaphor of "falling to bits" to describe the infant's feeling of disintegration, which, she wrote, was caused by internal persecutory feelings due to introjection or projection.

In the following section, I have selected some excerpts from the material that illustrate the theme of falling. I will speculate, using both "languages", about what kinds of unconscious thoughts and feelings *falling* may have represented, and how various kinds of falling activities were seen to express and/or defend against anxiety.

## Excerpts from observational material

Anny told me she had fallen on the way home from nursery on the day of our second meeting; but it was during the fourth observation that I first witnessed her falling. She had a friend, Joe, visiting, and she was in quite a keyed-up state.

> Anny suggested that she and Joe go up to her room, and mother said it was okay. I followed them. Anny said, "We can be mummy and daddy," and initiated a game of jumping on the bed. She asked me if she was jumping very high. I said she was. She said she would try to touch the ceiling. She said she was going to jump to the sofa, which she

did. I felt nervous about this, but she seemed to know how to perform this daring trick. She said, "Where's my baby?" and picked up a small doll and climbed on the bed again. As Anny became more and more excited, her breathing became increasingly audible. Just as mother was heard to approach the door, Anny jumped and hit her head on the sofa arm. Anny began to cry. Mother warned Anny that this is what happens when she jumps like this, and told her to jump only up and down. Anny flopped on to her back on the bed and seemed very frustrated. She kicked her legs and hit the bed with outstretched arms in one quick gesture.

I felt there was something in the timing of the accident, the fall into space, which had to do with mother approaching the scene, as if Anny suddenly felt "caught in the act" and brought up short. The jumping had a definite sexual quality in which Anny could reach the heights, bridge the precarious gaps, and take possession of the baby. The momentum of these strivings was building toward a climax. Mother's entry into this excited, triumphant scene seemed to have the effect of replacing Anny's omnipotent phantasies with feelings of anxiety and guilt, obliterating her sense of space and direction, and bringing her down to earth with a thud. In the moment of the fall, bound flow replaced the direct focus in space needed to make a successful leap, as the flood of conflicting feelings intruded into her mental space. Anny then flopped down on her back expressing her frustration, using strong weight, sudden time and free flow—an exasperating moment of passion drive. This description provides a clear and vivid example of the way in which primitive phantasies were played out through Anny's physical expression in movement.

### "One fell out and then she was dead, roll over, roll over"

Two weeks later, an example of the alternating rhythm between Anny's very controlled actions and feelings and her nearly uncontrollable ones was enacted quite clearly. Mother's parents were visiting from Norfolk. I found Anny in the kitchen with Granny, who supervised closely as Anny painted at an easel. Anny carefully and deliberately painted "a tiger", using direct focus, light weight, sustained time—the qualities of gliding movements. Granny told me that Cora was unwell. Soon after, as she painted, Anny sang:

"Ten in a bed, the little one said roll over, roll over. One fell out, and then she was dead, roll over . . ." She put the paintbrush down. She scampered to where I was sitting and twirled around. She was over-excited.

Anny's destructive phantasies towards her sister seemed to be expressed in both her deliberate painting of a dangerous creature who could eat small children, and her unmistakably vicious song. In this case, the "falling" seems to relate to a phantasy of doing away with a rival. This was followed by a manic flight round the room, which was mainly characterized by free flow and sudden (accelerated) time—the mobile state—in which the sense of perspective and thought stimulated by the awareness of space and the sensory element of weight again recede to the background. The flight may have been to escape from both the guilt and persecutory anxieties associated with having had such murderous thoughts.

She then gathered herself together, slowing down (sustained time) and narrowing her focus (direct space)—components of the "awake state"—in order to play a board game with Granny. But during the game, which involved careful attention to rolling dice and moving her marker round the board (placed on the coffee table), she became increasingly preoccupied with other, more physical, activity.

> Anny was lying on the floor, extending her legs to the ceiling, levering herself with her legs on the table into an arch, then turning on to her tummy, flopping on to the floor. She kept up with her turn, dropping the dice with an extended arm. She started to increase her physical actions, levering her weight up on to the table and then rolling to her back on the floor, then standing and dropping backward on to a sofa. Granny asked if she wanted to go on with the game or stop. She said, "stop". Anny came and sat beside me. Suddenly she slid off the leather sofa and on to the floor. She laughed and came back and lay with her head near my knee and rolled off again.

In this sequence, we see a different combination of qualities in Anny's movement, neither highly controlled nor manic, as she explored being upside down, arching, leveraging her weight, and falling off of things. She was very physically engaged, activating her *weight*; and she seemed to be exploring (fluctuations in) *flow* and *space* as well. In the abruptness of falling or the sustainment of sliding down, she also explored her relationship to *time*. We could say she was more intensely involved in embodying her phantasies than in either the more manic or very controlled sequences. This time she explored feelings of being the one who slips away or is dropped, rather than visiting these thoughts on her sister. She may even have been trying out her phantasies about what birth is like, having perhaps had some awareness of an unborn baby being on the scene. These wide ranging preoccupations seem to take over from the part of her which could rein herself in and stick to the straight and narrow, so to speak, as happened when she identified with being "grown up".

### Selective attunement

The following week, the seventh observation, I noticed a lack of synchrony between Anny's wild exuberance and mother's ability to meet or attune to it.

> Anny rather suddenly began to skip-run round the table and round the room in a large circle. Mum said, "Take a rest, you're making us dizzy." Anny picked up her baby doll from the floor. She threw the doll down, then picked her up and ran round with the doll. Anny fell as she went round a corner, but again jumped up and seemed fine.

Keeping in mind that mother was preoccupied with being in the early stages of pregnancy, and perhaps quite concerned about holding on to this baby as she had already experienced one miscarriage, one can certainly understand her impulse to dampen down Anny's fast and furious performance rather than to applaud or embellish it. But mother's remarks had a rather monotone, detached quality, and thus, seemed in marked contrast to Anny's mood, as if it was not possible to let herself either follow along with Anny's excitement or to help Anny, either physically or vocally, to process or contain it. I wondered whether, in this state, Anny may have experienced mother as having neither a containing mind nor lap.

The trauma associated with mother's first miscarriage would undoubtedly have been aroused by her current pregnancy, perhaps giving rise to "numbing", which Tracey writes, "is a well documented response to trauma . . . recognized as having a physiological basis" (2000). The excerpt also brought to mind what Stern called "selective attunement" (1985), in which a mother attunes to those aspects of her child's behaviour that are felt to be more acceptable, while not attuning to other aspects. In the material so far, mother seemed more attuned to Anny when she channelled her energy into focused, controlled activity.

At the end of the sequence described above, Anny herself became a terribly hostile mother to her own baby, who got thrown down with force. This could be construed as an attack on her sibling or the unborn baby, or as a suicidal impulse as she turns the murderous feelings on her own baby self. In movement terms we see an intensely energetic moment, in which all four Effort elements seem active—the strong weight, sudden time and direct focus of a punch with the addition of highly emotive free flow.

### "My baby fell on her head"

By the last meeting before the Christmas break, a fortnight later, I had begun to suspect that mother's subtle weight gain meant that she was pregnant, though nothing had been said. When I arrived, Anny and mother were playing with a doctor's kit.

> Anny brought her baby to doctor mum. She said, "Doctor, my baby fell on her head." Mum sounded blasé when she said, "oh no, not again."

The theme of falling was uncomfortably familiar to them both. Mother's response seemed to reflect her weariness with being repeatedly confronted, one way or another, with the thought of a baby in danger of "falling through space".

My suspicions about pregnancy gained ground when:

> Anny lay down on the cushions. She said her tummy hurt from the other baby that was inside. She said she was going to have the other baby today. Then Anny slid, head first, off the sofa, and said, "I like to do that." She picked up the doll and threw her on to the floor and said, "She likes that!" She then slid off again. She kept moving round, and said the baby inside her was making her move like that. She said, "It hurts when she kicks me, but I don't say anything."

Variations on the theme of falling are repeated here: first Anny's exploration of either being the baby herself as she experiences sliding, or, perhaps, of actually trying out the idea of making space in her mind for a new baby to slide into the family. The former might have been thought of as primarily an internal "dream state" experience derived from the physical sensations of weight and the feelings associated with flow linked to becoming the inside baby. The latter would have also brought in a third element, that of the mental realm of space, which implies a three-dimensional triangular space with room for three-way relationship (Britton, 1998).

The violent throwing of a doll seems to convey Anny's being in the grip of either a vengeful, destructive or a violent, suicidal aspect of herself—or both. These outbursts of feelings, which unleash movement qualities of strong weight, sudden time and free flow—qualities of the spaceless "passion drive"—are quite split off from the part of her which identifies with a controlled and effective mother. As Anny speaks of not complaining about the internal baby's kicking, we also see an identification with a martyr version of mother. Here the implication is that Anny denies the physical sensations in favour of the thoughts and feelings associated with keeping things under control—qualities of the remote state as seen in mother.

### After the miscarriage

The first observations after Christmas coincided with the very day mother had had the miscarriage. She told me about it the following week, and said that "Anny thinks I had a tummy ache." On that occasion, Anny clearly seemed aware of a loss, which evoked manic and anxious responses.

> Anny said, "Can I put on my bride's dress?" Mum said okay, and went to fetch it. Meanwhile Anny climbed on to a chair and said, "Do you want to see my Daddy's bag?", taking a zipper bag from the table and placing it on the floor in front of my feet. She unzipped it and showed me inside. She put her hand in and touched the objects: toothpaste, energy bars, toothbrush. Hearing mum approach, Anny zipped the bag quickly. Mum carried a white dress and "veil". Anny scampered quickly round the dining room, changing direction randomly, which seemed over-excited and manic. Anny put the white dress on. Mum

called it her Cinderella dress and said, "It's her favourite thing at the moment." Anny asked for the crown and mum helped her put on the jewelled headband. Anny asked for the veil, which mum tried to clip on to the back of her hair. Anny looked at me with a big grin.

Anny's play at being the triumphant one, with access to the secret inside life of father, had a brittle and poignant quality. Her aimless, speedy "dance" betrayed the confusion of thoughts and phantasies she tried to keep split off. In movement terms, we again see the mobile state, motivated by fluctuations in time and flow, and lacking in stability. Mother seemed unable to help Anny to contain her omnipotent phantasies, but rather seemed to assist her in indulging them. Mother expressed her own anxiety by commenting on the high-heeled Barbie shoes Anny wore to complete her outfit. She warned her to take off her shoes on the stairs.

> Mum said, "They love these shoes but they can be so dangerous on the stairs. I can just see her falling down a flight of stairs and breaking her neck."

It was as if the threat of death was perilously close at hand; and perhaps mother was quite terrified of her own destructive capacity, feeling perhaps that death was a more powerful force than life and there was no way to keep things from falling. There was no container for either mother's or Anny's distress. Father's noticeable absence at home may have felt like an added loss for them both. The grief of all the family appeared to be well hidden.

In the following meetings, there were many instances of falling, flopping, and sliding. In February Anny again manically ran round and flopped on to sofas and took off running again.

> Mum warned her to be careful, to remember what happened yesterday. Anny stopped and told me she fell and hurt her knee and her lip bled a little. She went to the far sofa and flopped again. She sucked her thumb and watched me, as I watched her. Then Anny demonstrated how she slides slowly to the floor, extending her legs toward the ceiling as she goes. She did this twice.

The falling initially seemed to convey a manic splitting and denial of reality, as if a predator was chasing, and would catch her sooner or later. The flopping that followed seemed to represent a more depressive acceptance of real time and space, a giving in to weight and gravity. I felt this particularly in Anny's allowing a lonely baby part of herself to be seen and held by my observing gaze as she lay still on the sofa sucking her thumb. This felt like a timeless, spell-like moment between us, in which the elements of weight, space, and flow were all active. There was no need to rush away from feelings; rather, they could be embodied. The sequence depicts a transition from the two-dimensional paranoid–schizoid moment to the three-dimensional depressive position.

It was much later, in mid July, that Anny sustained her most painful and scary fall during an observation. Three weeks previously father, unusually, replaced mother at an observation. The reason was that mother "had a bad tummy ache", to quote Anny; father explained that she was going to hospital for a prenatal scan. I later surmised that a third miscarriage had occurred, though I never knew for certain. At the aforementioned July observation,

> Anny began to neatly colour in her picture of the "Barbie princess", then said, "I don't want to do this any more. I want to play Barbies. I have a new bride's dress." She got down from her chair and ran up the two steps to the dining room, but tripped and fell hard on to her tummy and looked at me with a horrified look before starting to cry loudly. She staggered to mum, who was in the foyer. Mum held her and calmly asked if she fell up the stairs on to her belly. Anny nodded. Anny continued to howl with mouth open wide. I knelt beside them in the small area. Mother asked Anny if she wanted to sit in the room while she changed Cora. Anny nodded. We went upstairs. She sat in the chair and continued to howl as mum, ever so calmly, changed Cora and talked to her. She again told Anny to try to stop crying, and it would feel better.

I was struck by the way the "tummy ache" suffered by mother and the brutal fall suffered by Anny coincided. Anny seemed to experience this fall as totally catastrophic. She seemed to be quite helpless, and looked to me desperately as one might in the face of death. Although there may have been persecutory phantasies, this fall seemed to represent more than that, as if the bottom had catastrophically fallen out of everything. I felt it was her way of responding to overwhelming and uncontained distress. It was striking that the manic need to bring in the bride, as seen after the first miscarriage, had been repeated here.

Although mother did try to contain Anny's terror afterwards, she again seemed to offer a somewhat numbed response. I was shocked when she implied that Anny's falling on these stairs was not an isolated incident. Just at the moment Anny thought of the bride and sprung into action, as if bursting free from an imprisoning accumulation of bound up emotional confusion and distress, she fell most painfully. The swirl of uncontained feelings could not really be expressed in the two-dimensional activity of colouring-in the princess; yet the burst into three-dimensional space with her intense unconscious anxiety about the miscarriages was not possible to embody either. Anny may have been terrified of annihilation herself and/or felt responsible for the lost babies.

Rhode (2002, p. 232) reminds us that both Bick and Tustin wrote that three-dimensional space, with its implication of separateness, can be associated with the terror of falling. In movement terms, in collapsing so completely Anny lost control of weight, and of being in both space and time, as if a surge of affect had attacked and incapacitated her. Mother's calm, remote state, her apparent lack of anxiety about Anny's condition, stood in marked contrast to Anny's screaming in pain, leaving me with the impression that Anny was expressing something for them both.

*Variations on the theme of falling*

During the period between the two miscarriages, roughly between observations 18–26, Anny often found the need to "poo" during the observations. Mother noticed this and commented, "It must be that time of day again."

Anny may have felt the observation time provided a container that allowed an exploration and a letting go of pent up thoughts, feelings, and physical sensations. Yet, it is also true to say that she felt quite ambivalent about just what I represented at times. Through projective identification, her intense persecutory feelings could become lodged in me. For example, in June:

> As I approached the kitchen door, the door slammed. Mum went to the dining room door as it was also about to be slammed and went

in, saying that it was not nice to do that. I caught sight of Anny as I entered the kitchen. She looked at me with a frown on her face, near tears.

Here is an example of how ambivalence is communicated in no uncertain terms through non-verbal expression. Once acknowledged or expressed physically, it may then be more easily thought about.

Overall, I would say Anny made very good use of the observations to deal with pressing anxieties. I would like to mention one more sequence, which occurred near the end of the one year period, in which the action of flopping down seemed to express a sense of relief, an integration and acceptance of depressive feelings. In October, Anny started school. I arrived to see her in her school uniform, going through a box of old toys and party favours, reminiscing about them with mother.

Anny asked mum if she could use her measuring tape and measure mum. Mum agreed. Anny asked sheepishly if mum could attach the tape to her uniform, which mum did. Anny then gave the end of the tape to mum who put it on her head and Anny took it to the ground but they both laughed as it was attached to Anny and hard to reach the ground. Anny said she would like to measure everything.

I had the feeling that these activities of revisiting the past, and getting the measure of things, actively connecting with mother, was a very positive experience, and expressed a coming to terms with reality, reasserting normality. It did have the quality of control and practicality, the "grown-upness" seen in early observations. The focus in space was, as before in this mood, very sharp (direct). Then Anny seemed to feel an urgency to change:

Anny said as she headed toward the door, "We're going to play upstairs now." I followed her. Mother stayed behind. When she got to her room, she climbed on to the bed, flopping on to her back. She lay there for a prolonged eyes-closed moment, with what seemed to be great relief. She then snapped out of it and said "We can play Barbies now." She got up and went towards the shelf, singing. But she abruptly started to walk backwards in circles, her head initiating, almost out of control. This led into flopping backwards on to the bed again, where she looked at me upside down. She laughed and stood and dropped to the floor before repeating the backward walking. I felt she was releasing much pent-up expression.

The falling in this sequence seemed to have none of the quality of a traumatic collapse described earlier as "falling through space". Perhaps the measuring-tape play with mother supported a recognition of both their connection and their separateness, a way of defining the real and appropriate distance between them. This in turn may have afforded Anny a sense of boundaried safety and an ability to relinquish her defences—both the tight control of feelings and the rushing away from them.

Her backward circling was different from movements I had ever seen her do. Anny was actually taking a big step forward in her life, in entering the exciting unknown of school. I thought her backward walking and flopping may have stood for a recapitulation of events of the past year, allowing herself to fall back, without fear of disintegration—but rather, in order to absorb the chaotic experiences, to put them into perspective and to recover. At least for the moment, I felt Anny had found and internalized the containment she needed for this to happen.

## Summary

Joyce McDougall has written "The body speaks no known language, yet it serves, time and again, as a framework for communicating the psychic scenes of the internal theatre" (McDougall, 1986, p. 53). In this family's drama, the miscarriages this mother suffered during and before the year I observed her daughter seemed to turn Anny's normal Oedipal anxieties into more catastrophic anxieties (Bick, 1986).

Mother's own preoccupations seemed to mean that her containment of Anny's feelings was necessarily somewhat constrained. Mother may have unconsciously felt Anny's falls as persecutory actions, uncomfortably reminiscent of miscarriage. Anny responded defensively to mother's limited containment primarily in two ways—through the use of excessively controlled activity, or through taking flight in an aimless or triumphant frenzy, which often resulted in a fall.

Anny quite creatively and constructively explored anxieties and phantasies about the lost babies through various kinds of falling—from the sudden and scary collapse to the slow sliding off, or flopping on to, furniture. Some activities expressed the mourning associated with loss and the depressive position, others the splitting off of persecutory feelings, associated with the paranoid–schizoid position, and others were of the very primitive, passive type, as if falling into an abyss.

I hope to have made clear that it was not only the use of symbolic play which helped Anny to explore feelings, but the actual physical act of embodying feelings and phantasies, exploring them using her whole body in time and space. The sometimes subtle changes from one state to another were rendered describable using LMA.

My own body helped to contain her by providing a "resonating chamber" through which I could receive her states of mind. This deepening of attention to both my own bodily experience as the observer and the child's bodily expression lays the groundwork for greater awareness of *psychophysical* manifestations of transference and countertransference processes in patient–therapist relationships.

# CHAPTER EIGHT

# The social arena of the nursery

"Links are established between internal and external reality, in an ongoing 'weaving' process that gives meaning to the self and the world, and to the self in the world"

(Maiello, 2000, p. 6)

T he young children discussed in this short chapter were, like Anny in the previous chapter, three and four years old. I observed them at a nursery school on a one-hour weekly basis for four months. The setting interested me greatly, as these children were making their first forays into the social arena, experiencing feelings associated with autonomy, and being in a group of peers without the usual kind of parental supervision. There were around sixteen children in the nursery and two female teachers, supported by one or two mothers who attended on a rotational basis.

Bowlby writes about his observation of young children: "They show with unmistakable clarity how early in life certain characteristic patterns of social behaviour—some hopeful, others ominous—become established" (1988, p. 91). In considering the issues facing the various children from both psychoanalytic perspective and in terms of their movement profiles, it was clear that characteristic movement qualities reflected the mental and emotional states of the various children. The children's internal worlds of object relations were brought to bear on their interaction with each other and with the contents of the space.

## Two modes of communication

For these children, as for Anny, the language of movement, derived from direct physical and emotional experience, was no longer the primary mode of expression. Verbal language extended the possibilities of their symbolic play and the derivation of meaning, to include the representation of reality based on wishes and memories. Stern was of the opinion that, "With the emergence of language, infants become estranged from direct contact with their own personal experience. Language forces a space between interpersonal experience as lived and as represented" (Stern, 1985, p. 182). Implicit in the use of language is the possibility of distorting and transcending reality. But I believe we saw how Sam, in Chapter Five, was able to distort and transcend reality without access to language. Language, we can say, provides the means to elaborate and firm up a narrative to overlay the primitive preverbal "story".

Because language in these young children was newly acquired, I felt that the preverbal aspect of their expression was still a considerable feature of their play. They had not yet learned to privilege verbal communication or to curtail their physical expressivity to the extent that school-age children quickly learn to do. It could be said that verbal language communicated the "what", and movement communicated the "how". In adult communication, more credence is given to the "what". But perhaps another, perhaps deeper, layer of truth can be found in the "how". Bateson coined the term "double bind messages" to describe what happens when verbal and non-verbal messages clash (Bateson, 1972).

With the acquisition of language mental and emotional links are made. Thoughts are realized. This includes the ability to negotiate Oedipal issues and further the development of separateness, difference, and absence. But Urwin reminds us that Stern also emphasized that the gains provided by language were counterbalanced by the loss of the "intimacy provided by pre-verbal communication" (Urwin, 2002, p. 74).

## The nursery environment

I felt the nursery provided a very challenging environment for many of the children. From my first visit, I became aware of the high level of anxiety in the setting. The predominant groupings seemed to centre round a dominant male, Frank, and a dominant female, Nina. For both of these children, the urge to project their own unacceptable feelings into other group members was strong; and there was no shortage of children ready to receive these projections in exchange for a secure place alongside the leaders. How much the children's strivings were reflections of internal struggles, relating to issues whose origins lay in preverbal experiences, is open to speculation. A few children were able to use the nursery's resources creatively, oblivious to the cliques and pecking orders.

## Frank's sphere of influence

On my first visit,

> I observed in the kitchen area, where four children were playing—three boys and a girl. The clear central figure was Frank, who was taller than the others. He was rolling playdough with a rolling pin, very vigorous and efficient, with clear intention and attention to the task. He said he was preparing a fish. Two other boys leaned passively against the table watching. Their arms hung limply at their sides. One asked, "Does the fish talk?" "No," Frank shouted, "it's dead." Frank added more play-dough and pressed hard to roll it in with the rest, saying he was adding some nice vegetables for a fish pie. The other boys seemed in thrall to Frank as they stood, inert and passively watching.

With this pronouncement, it almost seemed that the other children felt at risk of being blotted out entirely by Frank's authoritative presence.

Frank referred to his wife, Gwen, and the girl who stood quietly beside him suddenly beamed. She was putting some playdough into a pan; but her attention was not fully on the task as she, like the others, was impelled to watch Frank.

It is as if Frank and only Frank could assert himself, and have an impact. His natural high level of vitality attracted the adhesive attention of followers, who seemed to fulfil his need to have his abilities admired, and unchallenged. In movement terms, we see Frank using strong weight, direct focus, and sustained time, as exemplified in his pressing the dough. His movements were integrated and effective. The flow of his imagination was evident, too, in his ability to symbolize. The energy of the other two boys, Eddie and Carl, seemed depleted. Like the fish, they seemed to carry feelings of lifelessness.

Frank ran outdoors and went to play with the cars. His two cohorts followed, as did Gwen. She went to the paints and as I came near she took all four brushes at once, glanced at me, then used them as a bunch in circular movements making a muddy brown colour. When she finished, she removed the apron and went to Frank. She held his left arm and pulled him. He ignored her. She was persistent, but was clearly rebuffed. She let go and seemed quite sad.

I wondered if Gwen clumped the four brushes together as a representation of the four children mucking in together, in an attempt to deny her gender difference; as if by being one of the boys she might be more accepted by Frank.

Upon leaving the nursery at the end of a session, I noticed Frank being greeted by his mother. She was carrying a baby sister, and mother and baby wore dresses with the same floral fabric. I felt that Frank felt doubly sidelined, not only by a new sibling, but one who was twinned with mother. Perhaps any dependent, "babylike" feelings of his own were strenuously denied and located, through projective identification, firmly inside the children who revolved round him. Contrary to first impressions, Frank probably needed his admirers at least as much as they appeared to need him.

In time, Eddie became the key companion to Frank.

They wore unusual jumpers exactly alike. Eddie seemed to be showing how completely he identified with Frank. Carl, noticing this couple, made an effort to fit in by pointing out his shorts were the same colour; but this was to no avail.

Outdoors, I was drawn to watch Carl, who now seemed firmly left out. As Frank got going on his usual scooter, and Eddie duly followed him, taking the only other one, Carl seemed lost and despairing. He stood at the doorway, holding his arms in a twisted way, close to his sides, so that his palms faced outward, by rotating his arms inward. He stood like that for about fifteen seconds. I sensed his intense anxiety. He then held his sweatpants by the elastic waist, tucking his fingers into the elastic at the side, then at the back. Then he held his long shirt at the sides and flapped it up and down several times. I thought this contact with his clothes was soothing him, but he also seemed in a daze or worse, a nightmare.

Carl, in his twisted arm movement, seemed to be trying to turn himself inside out in an attempt to disappear. He seemed to find himself abandoned by both his internal and external objects. He was gripped by bound flow and the mentally based element of space, leaving him frozen in the "remote state", lacking both weight and time to move him on or away. I felt he was captured for a moment by the desperate feelings that Bion characterized as "nameless dread" and which is also characterized by the split between mind and body. In this dissociated state, his life seemed to lose its meaning.

The sequence described above vividly illustrates how movement communicates primitive states of mind when words cannot. I could feel Carl's distress in my own body. In a therapy setting, the recognition of bodily experience, sensory and affective, by both patient and therapist can help to differentiate internal from external reality, and thus add insight into the process of reconciling past and present. The unconscious of all the children is revealed in a concrete way through the movement and gesture of the body, as the following continues to illustrate.

Later, when Jan wheeled the sand tray out, Carl went to stand between Frank and Eddie who pulled up on their scooters; Carl took a small corner space. I was struck by how he looked almost invisible. The other two looked bright and visible in the space while Carl seemed like an introverted shadow. He rested his hands on the plastic tray while the other two dug with spatulas.

It was as if Eddie and Frank formed a unit, enabling Eddie to now seem present in time, space and weight, albeit as adhesively identified with Frank. Carl had to carry the vulnerability for all three. As time went by, the configuration seemed to solidify. Carl seemed to drift away from Frank's sphere of influence, tending to play in a cut off space of his own. Compared to Frank, neither Eddie nor Carl seemed to have much ego strength. Eddie made do with living in the reflected glory of Frank; Carl faded into an anonymous space

Another boy, Billy, seemed impervious to the kind of sibling type rivalry seen in the others. True, one of his main pleasures was donning a superman cape and "flying" round the room—with sudden time and flexible space, an "awake state" attitude implying quick intuitive adaptation. One could describe this as a manic type defence. But even when in direct contact with the powerful Frank, Billy never showed signs of feeling restricted by him. He would not take in Frank's projections, which seemed at times to annoy Frank.

> Billy was at the sand pit with Frank, Eddie, and Carl. Billy had little sand but was shovelling what he had into a colander and enjoying watching it sift out. He tried to speak to Frank at various times, but Frank studiously ignored him. Though Eddie and Carl seemed stuck to their spots, Billy felt free to roam about the perimeter of the tray. He often responded to imaginative ideas of Frank's, but was never was acknowledged by him.

Billy's ability to keep a good, loving internal object alive, sustained him in his joy and creativity while he was being studiously ignored or rejected by Frank. Billy's movement vocabulary here consisted of light weight, sudden time and flexible space—the action of "flicking". In this way he was easily able to brush off the penetrating projections aimed at him by Frank.

We can assume that all the children were trying, through the roles they took on, to achieve a psychic equilibrium. The nature of their individual internal worlds dictated what kind of behaviour would offer a sense of safety. Frank's stature, his clearly defined goals, and his commanding self-confident persona gave me the feeling that he could become prime minister one day. Yet, as is often the case when watching political figures on television, I also suspected that were I to turn off the sound and watch in silence, I would see the shadow of Frank's vulnerability. "The unconscious is not an abstract entity", writes Resnik; "it is expressed concretely in the body" (1987, p. 70).

## Nina's charisma

Nina, the "head girl", also showed gang-like tendencies; she avoided anxious feelings by constructing a view of the world based on narcissism. She seemed to deny the authority of the nursery teachers, behaving as if she alone set the rules, as if she was the responsible, and glamorous, adult. The other girls were seen as possessing the incompetent, infantile qualities she pushed out. Lulu fully accepted this narrative. She strove to stick as close as possible to Nina, shadowing her every move.

> Lulu was tricycling behind Nina, riding right on her tail. Both girls rode fast. Nina was sitting tall, leaning slightly back, enjoying the pedalling and relishing the sensations and the sense of power; whereas Lulu leaned forward, pressing into her mission to follow.

The subtle yet striking differences in their movement qualities while riding tricycles seemed to convey the two girls' different states of mind. Nina had a lightness in her upper body and a flexible attitude towards space, (a combination within the stable state) as if the whole play yard was her kingdom. She maintained, in contrast to this, a strong and sudden use of weight and time in her legs (near state). The sensitivity to the overview of space in the upper body contrasts with purposeful strength in the lower.

Lulu showed similar elements of "near state", but in her whole body, rather than only her legs; and the exaggerated degree of strong weight and sudden time conveyed a stubborn, immovable intention. When her focus was locked on to Nina, and the elements of space, weight, and time were all engaged simultaneously, the action had the quality of "punch"—strong weight, sudden time and direct focus.

The only times Lulu would take the lead would be to crash into the perimeter fence. I wondered if this was her way of dealing with the degree of envy she held inside. Perhaps these feelings were partly introjected from Nina, but they were no doubt exacerbated by the fact that like some of the others, Lulu had a new baby sister.

Nina stopped suddenly and went inside to get a doll. She strode so confidently, purposefully, arrogantly. She had an openness in the upper
body and chest, a regal presence. Lulu was left standing beside her trike
with a lost look, as if temporarily unable to mobilize herself. She had no
one to follow. When Nina returned, there was an argument in which she
told Lulu she didn't like her any more. Nina propped the blonde doll on
the frame and rode off. Lulu followed. When she got alongside she
asked, "You don't like me any more?" and Nina said, "NO!" Lulu pouted
and seemed anxious, unable to just turn her back on Nina, rejecting her
in kind. Instead she kept tailing Nina, as if there was no choice.

As with Frank, Nina's natural high level of vitality attracted the
adhesive attention of followers. Lulu's need for attachment, in fact
her whole identity, seemed to depend on Nina. Her compulsion to
follow had a stalker-like quality. Nina finally looked down her nose
with contempt at Lulu's dependence. This was expressed with a
clear, punch-like retort and stance. Yet Lulu could not put the
brakes on her driving forward momentum, an extreme expression
of the "near state" in which the use of time and weight reflected her
fixation. The ability to reflect, associated with space, was absent.

Nina was clearly a gifted girl with great vitality and charisma.
It seemed, however, that she did often exploit her gift, as narcissistic tendencies took over. The following excerpt shows her seeming
to enjoy her ability to tease and excite.

Nina yelled hello to some delivery men outside the fence, and was so
obviously pleased and excited when they returned her greeting that her
body seemed to vibrate. She then got off her trike and took off running
through the space, leaving Lulu stranded, while enticing several boys
to run after her by running close alongside them in a zigzag fashion.

Her movement qualities were the ones described earlier—a flexible focus in space, with a lightness in the upper body and a
strength in the lower body. Her approach to time was sudden. The
actions this created were flicks in the upper body, supported by
strong, sudden punch-like action in the lower. This split perhaps
conveyed something of the different parts of herself which inhabit
her internal "gang". The upper body's lightness and flexibility
could be seen as a more feminine aspect, while the lower body
strength and determination were more stereotypically masculine.

Her simultaneous embodiment of both gender characteristics may have contributed to her charisma. In fact, the same could be said of Frank, who was as at home in the kitchen as he was on the scooter. When Nina attempted to do something other than entice or frustrate others, rather, to create something in its own right, her efforts often went awry.

> Nina and Kira were at the playdough table. I was struck by how hard it seemed for Nina to make an impact on the dough as she used a rolling pin, whereas Kira was keenly involved in pressing it flat so she could cut gingerbread men. Nina had a huge mound of dough. She liked to lean her whole body on to it, lifting her legs off the floor as a way to make an impression on it. She did not seem to have any thoughts about what she was making. When Kira made a gingerbread man and placed it on the table and then made another, Nina took them both and mashed them into her mound. Kira looked distressed and shocked for a moment, and then she just got on with rolling more dough. Nina began to whinge loudly at not having enough. Kira looked at her with a concerned expression, seeming not to want to upset her, and/or afraid to challenge her.

The preoccupation with how she measured up to the others, and how to get rid of rivals, disallowed Nina from using her weight, focus, and timing productively. She could not bear to see creativity exist in others, because it challenged the narcissistic myth of being the only capable one, which she needed to maintain. Her pressing movement was not focused on making an impact on the clay; it seemed to represent a bound flow destructive phantasy directed at Kira's creativity. Kira was immune to the aggressive projection. She could sensitively employ a range of actions—pressing, dabbing, gliding movements—in her careful efforts to create something with a life of its own. She was centred within herself and could express a varied movement vocabulary, unlike Lulu, whose centre of attention resided not within herself, but within Nina, and whose limited movement vocabulary reflected her frustrating dilemma.

## Conclusion

I hope I have identified some of the issues that created such an anxious atmosphere within this group of children, who were not, in any obvious sense, deprived or threatened; but who were all faced with negotiating the delicate transition between fusion and separation. Their behaviour in the nursery betrayed internal feelings of anxiety that coloured their states of mind and body, feelings which, in all likelihood, had their roots in preverbal life experience.

As children create images of themselves in relationship with the world, they do so in ways that are definable in terms of both the psyche and the body. The recurrent physical patterns can, I think, be said to reflect internal object relations, and to underlie both the children's verbal and mental patterns and the roles they assumed in the group. It was as if specific maps for social interaction and self perception were being established right there in the nursery, maps which, one imagines, could carry on into adulthood.

I was able to use my own embodied attentiveness to receive and monitor changes in the children's states, as well as using my mind to think about what was happening. In the next section, I illustrate how the primitive transference and countertransference processes perceived through embodied attentiveness are developed and worked with psychophysically in movement psychotherapy with individual adult patients.

# PART III
# CLINICAL CASE STUDIES

# Introduction

I n the following three chapters I apply the synthesis of psycho-analysis and movement analysis to my work with three patients in clinical movement psychotherapy. The key difference between the clinical material and the observational material in Part II is that here I use and discuss the importance of the transference and countertransference, and how the two frameworks together may provide a broadening and deepening of their experience.

I illustrate how the object relations framework may enhance theoretical underpinnings in DMT, and demonstrate how embodied attentiveness to psychophysical states may help psychotherapists and their patients engage more consciously with non-verbal experience. I also provide examples from case material that suggest that the kinds of psychophysical patterns discussed in the infant and young child observations can be perceived in movement therapy to underlie patterns in adulthood.

The setting for this work is a small, light studio with a wooden floor. The room is empty except for folded blankets at one end of the room, provided for the patient and myself to sit on, and one large plant in a corner.[1] The blankets are angled so that they face diagonally into the space. But each patient makes use of the space and the blanket in his/her own way, and this can be seen to have implications for exploring patients' internal object world.

## Note

1. Since writing this material I have added a few simple props, such as balls and cushions, for patients to make use of as they wish.

# CHAPTER NINE

# "I don't know where I come from"

"To tell a story is often to make images . . .
We cannot take a step in life or literature without using an
image . . . Not only does each image tell its singular story,
but that story invokes another"

(Hardy, 1975)

This chapter looks at the interrelationships between psychic and somatic processes with a particular theme in mind—this concerns the way in which visual imagery entered the free associative process of a very imaginative and articulate patient in movement psychotherapy. Specifically, I illustrate the different ways in which imagery was mobilized by Francine, a woman in her mid-twenties.

It became clear to us both that, although her movement was a catalyst for copious and vivid visual images, and she put these into words clearly and freely, images sometimes served to abruptly distance her from her sensory and affective experience in the here and now. At these times the images seemed—while certainly adding something to the experience— also to provide an outlet, a place from which to disengage from embodied feelings and sensations, to muse intellectually. There were other times, increasingly frequent as the work progressed, when Francine's proclivity for imagery had the symbolic capacity to support psychosomatic integration, rather than diverting her attention and energy away from embodied feelings.

I shall explore these different uses of imagery in terms of their signalling, in the first instance a splitting and discontinuity between mind and body, and in the second, a way of supporting a more embodied containment of thoughts and feelings. I also consider whether and how the former has a resonance with two-dimensionality and the latter with three-dimensionality, considering both Rudolf Laban' s and Donald Meltzer's ideas on the subject of the relationship between the psyche and the geometry of space. Finally, I reflect on the use of my countertransference to register the different uses made of the imagery, as well as to foster a growing recognition of the difference by the patient, thus facilitating her ability to embody the images, and to let them move her. These themes will be explored with reference to material drawn from notes made after each session.

Bodily movement itself can be said to create images and to communicate non-verbally. Movement in this sense speaks for itself. But finding words to describe the sensory and affective experience, in the spirit of free association, is integral to my working process in movement psychotherapy. What is of interest is the potential for one mode of perception, in this case the kinaesthetic sense (of movement), to stimulate and promote the integration with other modes of perception which in turn re-stimulates the kinaesthetic sense, and so on.

Susan Isaacs wrote that the earliest and most rudimentary phantasies were bound up with sensory experience, as "affective interpretations of bodily sensations", noting that these served the purpose of giving "a concrete, bodily quality, a me-ness, experienced in the body" (Isaacs, 1952, p. 96). These most primitive of phantasies were differentiated from what she called "images in the narrower sense", which are representations *in the mind* of external objects. The former were related to the oral impulse to take in, to be nourished, and preceded the clear distinction between the inner and outer worlds.

For Francine, the facility for movement to evoke visual images was quite automatic. She would hardly have begun to move when she would be reminded of an image—often having reference to her childhood, her extensive travels or to literature. We investigated the timing of these associations as well as the images themselves, and their propensity, at times, to interrupt a flow of energy, obstructing Francine's ability to just let things flow. Why had she felt compelled at particular moments to step outside her experience and look from a different perspective as a way of assigning meaning?

The vivid collage of images stored in her memory often sprang to the surface like picture postcards delivered from the past. It became apparent, however, that as well as illuminating the material, these "postcards" had the effect of leading us away to other worlds rather than energizing or adding to the present exploration. On the other hand, her *associations* to the images could be quite meaningful at times.

As the images often seemed to represent snapshots of places Francine had lived, it is important to explain that she began her world travels at the age of two, when her family emigrated to India. She returned to Europe at age ten, only to feel totally uprooted from the culture to which she had become accustomed. She lived in three different European countries before training in international law in America. During holidays she took the opportunity to do volunteer work in various parts of South America, where she met and later married a fellow European. Her interest in, and practice of, dance from different cultures led her to seek a form of therapy that included movement.

Francine once said to me, "I don't know where I come from." I felt that as well as her obvious lack of a stable place to call home, her impulse to take leave of the here and now reflected her difficulty in knowing what it is like to be "at home" in the presence of another, to feel contained in a safe space in which she could allow physical sensations and feelings—at root perhaps, to feel at home in her own body. Laban's dream state, comprised of weight and flow—that is, of sensations and feelings—was felt to be nearly intolerable at first. Even a momentary experience of this internally focused state would be followed by a reactive jump to the opposite position, awake state, driven by space and time; through thinking and decision she could recover a needed, if anxious, feeling of control.

I wondered if Francine's early exposure to so many different and exotic images from the outside world in early childhood may have flooded her, making her unable to process them all or locate where she herself was in relation to the whirl of images. Did the exposure to so much in the external world make the images difficult to integrate, and therefore to achieve a sense of balance between the external world and the more internal, sensoriaffective phantasy life Isaacs describes? If this indeed was the case, it may have also been contributed to by the occurrence of a traumatic event suffered by the family around the time of Francine's birth.

Francine informed me in the first meeting that just before she was born, her maternal aunt had committed suicide; Francine felt that in mother's mind she was linked with this aunt. "As if she expected suicide of me. She told me I looked like my aunt and she gave me many of her things. I felt close to my aunt because of this."

She spoke of feeling either "overwhelmed" in the sessions or of fearing overwhelming me, as if we were both experienced alternatively as dangerously powerful, or defenceless and porous. Which one of us was perceived as the powerful and intrusive object at any moment and which was the vulnerable victim seemed to see-saw. The sense of bodily containment was hazy; the various parts of the personality were not felt to be held together by a containing skin (Bick, 1968).

It seemed possible that the family's sad and shocking loss may have meant that mother was too overcome by her own feelings to be able to provide the secure containment that Francine, as an infant, would have needed. Therefore, she may not have been able to develop the kind of "taking in" that would have allowed the sensorial and affective feelings and phantasies, which lay the groundwork for establishing an embodied sense of self, to take root and develop naturally. This could be thought of as the opposite of psychosomatic symptoms, in which mental life is transferred into bodily symptoms.

*Postcards from the past: diversion from, or transition to, feelings?*

Although the profusion of images seemed to inform the movement, much like associations to a dream, they also had the effect of distancing Francine from the emotional impact of feeling her body in movement. In the countertransference I sensed a split between mind and body in Francine, and often also in myself. In the second session:

> She is sitting, swaying side to side. She says it feels good, adding that she feels she is spreading her wings as the swaying increases; but as soon as the association is made the movement loses its energy. I am aware of a flat feeling in myself—my own thought is of broken wings. She then raises and lowers her arms perfunctorily in a vertical axis, saying that her hands feel like hayforks when they are on the ground and when in the air like "inverted Indian stupas".

She seemed to have withdrawn her attention from the sensation of her hands and arms and any contact with feelings; instead she had, in effect, attached herself to the visual images. These were often seen to represent memories.

> She associated hay forks with France, and a melancholy feeling, though these feelings were not much in evidence in the present. She told a memory of being ten years old, just having moved from India to France. Mother was sunbathing in the garden. She was beside mother and feeling very sad in this new environment. She wondered if mother felt this too; she thinks she might, but cannot ask.

Leuzinger-Behleber describes memory as "a function of the whole organism", a complex process that is based on actual sensory–motor experiences. She says, "memory is not an abstract cognitive function but embodied and as such a property of the entire organism" (Leuzinger-Behleber & Pfeifer, 2002, p. 5). I felt that in this case the memories that were stimulated in response to the images did in fact lead Francine to a *memory* of embodied feelings; but these feelings did *not* appear to hold much psychophysical resonance for her in the present. The initial images arose as an abrupt and disjointed move away from sensations and feelings. Her predominant state of mind as she described the images was "awake", motivated by space and time, the mental and the temporal. This would suggest that although memory may be based on sensory-motor experience, the recall of images may at times be employed as a way of fragmenting or distancing from that embodied aspect of memory.

The associated memories did, however, prove to be fruitful and relevant for thinking about the transference. It was possible to discern from them that Francine perceived me as both self-absorbed and vulnerable; and that she both wanted to be close and feared it. When the transference was recognized, Francine was able to feel these things as well as think about them, drawing on and integrating the internal world (sensing and feeling) and the external world (time and space). It seemed that as she was able to make further associations to the initial images, she could begin to embody the realm of feeling. She could become psychophysically "in-formed", rather than merely delivering "information".

## Double breathing

At times Francine complained of a feeling of constraint round her throat and difficulty in breathing. On a number of occasions she experienced what she called "double breathing", which she located in her throat.

> She says she can hear breathing, but that she isn't actually breathing. She associated this with her aunt. When I enquired about the method of suicide, she said she was pretty certain her aunt had hanged herself.
>
> She began to move her arms in an angular way, saying she felt like a shadow puppet. I was struck by the image because she seemed to be holding her breath and appeared somewhat two-dimensional. I was aware of my own held breath and tense belly. I asked about her breathing. She said it was shallow. She said she felt she wanted to sing, and put a hand to her upper chest. When there was no sound forthcoming, I wondered if she had a sense of what the sound would be like, if she could hear it in her imagination. She said, "A small wail." She did quick torso movements side to side from this chest point and noticed a breathy sound there. She asked if I could hear it. She said it was the double breathing. It seemed to both alarm and excite her.

I had the feeling that Francine felt both "possessed" by a suicidal internal object, and at the mercy of her own murderous feelings towards both mother and myself. As a way of keeping these dangerous feelings at bay, she kept her body held, as if flattened into a two-dimensional shape. It was as if, for Francine, giving in to gravity, breathing into an internal three-dimensional bodily space, or using her body in a strong and robust way, or even letting her "full tone of voice" come into the space (Mori, 2001), risked either unleashing internal objects capable of violence or killing off damaged ones. The feeling of letting things flow more freely and feeling at home in herself was longed for, but not easily attained. It was not surprising that another factor in Francine's seeking therapy was a history of amenorrhoea.

Attending to the subtleties of one's own and patients' breathing patterns can usually reflect significant changes in non-verbal, often unconscious attitudes experienced in the transference and counter-transference.

## A turning point

After several months of work, there seemed to be a turning point in Francine's ability to allow herself to explore the embodiment of her feelings with me. She commented at the beginning of a session that all week she had been thinking about the way I had leaned my body against the wall in the previous session, saying that I looked so relaxed. I do on occasion move to change my position or follow a patient's change of level, to lie or to stand. This feels necessary at times in order to stay present with my own psychophysical experience as well as the patient's; it can be a conscious or unconscious response to the countertransference. On this occasion I had not even written in my notes about this move to the wall, which had so struck Francine. Yet the sight of me being so "at home" that I could relax against the wall had obviously made a deep impression on her. Looking back at my notes, I distinctly remembered when my move had happened, though I am sure my decision was not made consciously. In fact, I remembered thinking to myself "what are you doing?" as I felt myself in an awkward slouch. The session she refers to began as follows.

> She says she still has mixed feelings about coming here. She crawls out into the space and does some perfunctory movements. I comment on the difficulty of knowing what to do, when there are these mixed feelings. She notices her held breath. She refers to "double breathing", just

at her throat, which she also felt when she woke today. She swings her arms forward and back and remarks herself on the flat shape of the movement. I feel the constraint in my own body.

She comments on sending a card to her family, with a picture of the changing of the guard. She felt anxious but sent it as a joke. When I ask for associations to the changing of the guard she said, "Who's guarding who?", saying she is fearful of a suicidal mother, that mother also guards her; father guards them both, and brother watches everyone. I'm aware it is hard, with all the internal objects on guard, for her to move spontaneously. The movements seem to be cut short.

It was at this point I remember sliding backward a few inches in my seated position in order to lean my weight against the wall. I think I was responding to and freeing myself from the stiff and vigilant soldier quality in Francine; I felt she was closely guarding me—I could be regarded as suicidally vulnerable or as sadistically threatening—as well as guarding herself, within whom these possibilities were also felt to lurk. I think my comfortable slouch expressed my own loosening of the rigid posturing. I was bringing an experience of weight and free flow into the space by embodying the physical and emotional realms, as I let gravity effect me. Then, perhaps affected by my own change of position, she seemed to come back down to earth, receiving her own weight.

She seems to relax a bit into the floor and says she can breathe now. She begins to roll, saying, "I feel like rolling all round the floor." She pushes into and out of the floor. She says she loves the spinal pattern as she continues rolling.

The spinal pattern she referred to is a sequential twisting rotation through the spinal bones, which required much more physical involvement of the whole body than did the previous, more peripheral, arm swings. She had begun to mobilize her weight, by both pressing into the floor and creating three-dimensional shaping movement in her torso.

I remark on her real relationship with the floor and she seems to recognize it too. She levers her body off the floor by pressing one hand down, suspending her torso, opened out away from the floor. It creates an arc-like shape. She says she loves this especially. I ask what she loves about it. She says the way the head leads but the spine follows. It reminds her of a Japanese temple. I remark on the way the head and the body are connected and energy is flowing. She says she also has an image of a sword. I remark on the way she cuts the flow abruptly when she reaches a certain tolerance level. She agrees. She speaks of feeling nauseous as if it is suddenly a bit too much to digest.

Here Francine seemed to be able to allow herself to inhabit both her body's internal space and feel contained in the external space by me, and it seems to have had something to do with my slouching against the wall. She expressed her love for a particular stretching movement, which may also have been her way of expressing her love for the work we were doing together—connecting the head and the body, so to speak.

She begins to move again, crab-like walking on hands and feet with her torso facing the ceiling, and then more rolling through the space. She says she feels the energy is building. She keeps going, without pauses or slowing. She says she recognizes anxious feelings in the movement and she fears if she slows down she will just go into her head. I inquire into these feelings. She says she feels aggressive. Moving on, she tells me how she got really angry and yelled at mother during the break. That it had felt good. That mother became more life size—not a huge monster.

In the foregoing description she was beginning to allow feelings to flow more freely. This session seemed to mark a turning point, at which Francine was able to recognize that it could be a relief to express and embody her feelings in my presence, that she could let herself feel somewhat at home in the therapy space. Rather than experiencing her physical sensations as threatening intrusions, imposed on her either by an internal object or by me, she was able to embody them as parts of herself, without distancing herself by grabbing hold of an image. She seemed to be recognizing that internal objects can be explored in therapy, that they can also recover and "become more life size".

## Psychophysical dynamics of infancy

As mentioned previously, it seemed quite likely that Francine's mother was preoccupied by her own sister's sad and shocking death around the time of Francine's birth. Therefore, it may not have been possible for her to properly attune to Francine's needs or to contain a lively, free flowing baby. Joyce McDougall suggests that in such situations

> certain highly charged emotional thoughts, which the mother cannot bear, become forbidden thoughts for her child. In the same way, certain bodily zones and certain physiological functions may not be contemplated or must be rendered devoid of pleasure because of the manner in which they are invested by the mother. [McDougall, 1989, p. 47]

If something similar had happened in Francine's case, it would go some way toward explaining her need to guard against too much sensoriaffective experience. It is possible that the process of containing projections may even have been reversed—rather than the expected maternal role of containing and transforming her infant's projections, this mother may have needed Francine to contain her own distress.

Francine was very strong in the Laban arena of attention to *space*, the mental aspect of experience. This could be thought of as her way of creating a "second skin" protection, the roots of which, as has been suggested, stretch back to infancy. Esther Bick refers to babies' holding on to objects with their eyes as one way of compensating for poor emotional holding (Bick, 1968). Francine's exposure to a whole new visual world at age two would have provided ample diversion from the primary experience of living in her body filled with uncontained feelings and sensations. Her ill-defined physical sense meant that her sense of boundaries was also ill-defined.

## Moving towards ending

Leading up to the Easter break, and knowing that we were to finish at the end of the summer term as Francine would be leaving London, the boundaries around the setting and the work were felt by her to tighten and to impinge. She had told me she "used to love flying, being in the in-between place, leaving things behind", but that now she did not feel so ready to leave things. This attitude seemed to be reflected in a greater sense of bodily awareness and discomfort. It seemed Francine was increasingly in touch with where she was coming from, so to speak, and not only where she was going.

> She says she'd like to start moving, that something is trapped and nervous. She kneels facing me at an angle. She says it feels like her muscles are like a coat, too tight, but also supportive. I sense she means that's how it feels here She turns away and lies on her belly and moves her elbows on the floor. She says, "That's an awful sound." I ask what about it. She says the sound of her bones meeting the floor. She puts her head to the floor, says she feels she's burying herself, then describes finding a centipede shell in the woods and burying it under leaves. A creature with lots of legs, not a caterpillar because it has no head. She puts forehead to floor. I inquire about this primitive creature, all segmented, no head, and her wanting to bury it or hide it away, as if she may want to protect or hide something of herself that feels like this.

Here is another example of a patient's ambivalence, about me and our work, being explored non-verbally, in her elbow movement. With hindsight, I see I did not take up the transference directly; but it is indirectly included in the following.

> With cheek to floor, she makes cooing sounds. She speaks of the animal with segments and how it is different from the "sequencing". I sense a mixture of fluidity and awkwardness in her body and in my own; and I ask if she feels both the segmented bits and the sequencing in her body. Yes, she says. She says her whole core is on the floor. She stays in reflective silence for some time.

In this sequence, the use of imagery felt much more embodied, and descriptive of ambivalent feelings. Perhaps Francine's thoughts about the break and ending affected what took place. She got down to the bare bones, so to speak. She could be present with and contain primitive feelings, and feel the potential for an all-joined-up sense of herself depicted by the idea of sequencing, where one thing naturally leads to another, and where mind and body are interconnected. She did not seem impelled, or perhaps able, to move at the end; she was present with her feelings in anticipation of separation, rather than flying off. This was a poignant experience for us both. Cheek to floor, she seemed to acknowledge support from and love for the therapy space.

The foregoing description illustrates the potential of including bodily experience in therapy work, to make embodied contact with primitive experience. We see how archaic patterns were felt to have reached the end of their useful life, to be replaced by more alive "sequencing" of experience. The shell could be lovingly buried and laid to rest.

In the last term of work, Francine's imagery became increasingly integrated with her feelings and her movement. A "crab without a shell", "a flower blowing in the wind, not going anywhere", "insects coming above ground" and a "powerful snake" were used not to evade but to recognize and name feelings. They seemed to represent an alive body, full of sensations. Passionate movement through space and aggressive, "messy" feelings were allowed out.

On one occasion these were linked with an image of dust flying in Africa when women beat their carpets, dust which turned a deep red when water was splashed on it. She associated this image with fertility. This seemed to metaphorically herald her announcement at the following session that her period had restarted. Near the end she spoke of an image of dancing with a partner, "maybe it's you". Francine made a considerable journey during therapy, internally rather than externally, which essentially allowed her to embody rather than take flight from her feelings and to salvage a damaged internal object world. Some months after finishing, she wrote to inform me she was pregnant, and I was included in a group email to receive the joyous announcement when her son was born.

### Being in space

Francine's development has been described as a progressive deepening of integration between mind and body, or as Thomas Ogden poetically described it—"a greater sense of being alive in the experience of a coextensive minded body and bodied mind" (Ogden, 2001, p. 174).

This was seen to have been reflected in a change from a two-dimensional sense of self, where images had a dull postcard-like flatness, to a much more three-dimensional presence. Over time, as she was able to tolerate the more primitive aspects of her experience, she recognized an internal space, a home ground, where sensations and feelings could co-exist with thoughts and imagination.

Laban described the body's orientation to space as having the dimensions of length, width, and depth; he felt that "harmonious" and integrated human movements created patterns that transit through all three-dimensions, usually moving from the centre of body to the periphery. Two-dimensional movement was associated with learned rather than natural movement (Maletic, 1987, p. 165).

The vertical dimension, linked to weight and thus to gravity, was initially the least developed in Francine. Her preference for time and space, components of the awake state—with their affinities with the sagittal and horizontal dimensions, respectively (also corresponding to the two-dimensional "wheel" and "table" planes, see Chapter Two)—was reflected in her wish to travel far and wide. But this was accompanied by a weak sense of her own vertical axis and sense of self at the "core" of her own journey.

In describing two-dimensionality from a psychoanalytic perspective, Donald Meltzer speaks of a "thinness of emotionality" which is a consequence of a "surface to surface relationship with objects". "Until the containing functions have been introjected, the concept of a space within the self cannot arise" (Meltzer, 1975b, p. 231). This description supports and augments Laban thinking about Space Harmony, and provides another meaningful context within which to consider Francine's journey in therapy.

To conclude this chapter I would like to refer to Ogden's suggesting that a baby is in no rush to be "minded" because mother is "minding him". He speaks of a "premature, defensive mindedness which is disconnected from bodily experience" (Ogden, 2001, p. 220). It is this type of early patterning that I think could well have been at the roots of Francine's protective attachment to the use of imagery.

Ogden (1997, p. 226) points out the paradox that it is mother and baby "living an experience together" that actually serves to create separation between them. For Francine, this process was facilitated by bringing her images into the therapy space. Though at first they were used to block or substitute for a playful exploration involving the overlap between the inner and outer worlds, as we "lived them together" they came to be used as springboards for discovering this overlap, and the recognition of both shared and separate psychic and physical realities.

In the next chapter I introduce a patient who, unlike Francine, knew much about where she came from, but had difficulty in contemplating where she could possibly be going.

# CHAPTER TEN

# "I don't know where I'm going"

"I have come to think that a sense of bodily separateness is the heartbreak at the centre of all human existence, and that for various reasons some people experience it in a more drastic way than others"

(Tustin, 1990, p. 166)

The struggle to achieve a balance between connectedness and separateness was the core issue in the work with Beth over four and a half years. I first encountered Beth, an art therapist in her early thirties, in a movement workshop I led. She wanted to explore movement as another creative medium, and having found the workshop meaningful, she asked about individual work. She had impressed me as a strong and embodied young woman who enjoyed moving. I would have characterized her preferred movement qualities in Laban terms, as weight (intention) and time (decision), which comprise the "near state". She seemed purposeful in her strong rhythmic movement; though, in hindsight, I can recall that she was not particularly attentive to the space or the others in the group, nor was she particularly connected to her feelings.

As we began our journey of once-weekly therapy, it became evident that, although Beth did have a powerful and articulate body, there was a noticeable split between her sense of her body and her sense of herself. There was a need to restore a link to an affectively experienced body, and also to support her in finding the words for describing her experience at this level. This meant giving up, for a while, her proficiency in movement, in order to make contact with the underlying feelings that the movement, it became clear, served to cover over. Beth's proclivity for bodily sensing could serve to provide her with an escape from feelings. Beth recognized a need for balance and integration; it prompted her to seek therapy. I, on the other hand, had to learn about the split as we embarked on the journey.

There was a part of Beth, I was to discover quite quickly, that yearned to *stop* moving, to slow things down to a standstill, to allow the submerged but pressing infantile feelings to surface. The first year of work was characterized by an atmosphere of strong infantile feelings, as if a one-to-one, mouth-to-breast, or even pre-birth relationship, was being recreated. The sessions had a timeless quality in the sense of *progression through* time; though there was a strong sense of *body time*, as experienced in the ongoing rhythm of breathing and heartbeat. It could also be said that these early sessions had a somewhat mindless quality, in the sense that it was difficult to put thoughts and feelings into words; there was little space for reflection. However, the "the primitive but powerful preverbal communications that take place between mothers and tiny infants" (Alvarez, 1992, p. 4) could have been said to pervade the relationship at this stage.

In Laban terms, this state of mind is best characterized as "dream state", in which the elements of weight and flow predominate; although both were clearly present, I would say Beth's experience of the sensation of weight was predominant. The weight, rather than being active, strong, and rhythmic as in the near state described above, was experienced as light, almost passive, sensual, and sensitive. It seemed resonant of early infantile experience. It often felt as if her body was undifferentiated from mine, or even from the floor or the space. One of the earliest sessions produced the following.

Beth begins by lying on her back, staying there a long time, breathing deeply, eyes closed. I sense her weightiness, as her awareness seems to spread through her whole body. She rolls to her side and to her belly and to her other side, stopping in a twisted shape and breathing deeply there, very clear in her position. I am drawn to lie down myself, feeling as if gravity were getting much more forceful. I lie on my side, at the edge of the space, from where, out of the corner of my eye, I see Beth in the middle of the room; and my sensation of my weight and position intensifies. I begin to feel vulnerable, tentative. The atmosphere feels entirely timeless. She carefully extends an arm, then a leg, extending and folding one limb at a time like this. She can see me from her position. She says she is glad to be in contact with me, glad I can be there with her. Everything seems in slow motion . . .

In the countertransference there was a sense of both absorbing her feelings and sensations and of being absorbed by her, as if, as McDougall puts it, ". . . there is only one body and one mind for two people" (McDougall, 1989, p. 32).

By the end of the sequence described above, Beth did recognize my body as separate from hers, providing space to differentiate what was psychological from what was somatic. In this early stage of working with me, Beth's registering of her emotional experience was faint, as if just beginning to become conscious of an emptiness of self inside. Lynch has described this state of affairs as like a "negative snapshot, a bodily outline", not yet having developed fully so that the "emotional colour" can be registered (Lynch, 2000, p. 166). This emotional colour, or feeling tone, as it might also be called, is represented in Laban's language as *flow*.

The communication between us, body to body, as distinct from verbal communication, calls to mind the rather recent investigations in neuroscience that have shown that the human ability to "mirror" others' actions originates in the brain at a much deeper level than phenomenal awareness. A new class of neurons has been discovered in the premotor area of the brain, the so-called "mirror neurons". These are motor neurons that fire in response to observing motoric activity in another—they fire in the identical pattern, hence the term mirror. It is thought that this kind of interaction may shed new light on the functional architecture of conscious vs. unconscious mental processes (see Stamenov & Gallese, 2003).

Since all emotional work can be said to be intimately connected with the body, this work may have important implications for inter-action between therapist and patient, not only in movement therapy, where mirroring, often in a more literal sense, is a core process in the work, but in any therapeutic relationship. The consideration of what is required for a multi-dimensional experience of "mirroring" may become an increasingly important focus in transference–countertransference processes.

My decision to lie down was a communication in response to my "reading" of the situation, like my leaning against the wall with Francine. This kind of communication is readily available to move-ment psychotherapists. I am suggesting that greater attunement to non-verbal material may mean that this level of communication can be augmented in verbal psychotherapy or psychoanalysis, leading to a meeting of "bodyminds". Taking the mirror neuron work into account, might the use of the couch in psychoanalysis become open to debate, at least for some patients?

The following is an example from the sixth month of work, in which I am again intuitively drawn to move physically in order to be on Beth's level literally, as it were. It often felt during this period that by joining Beth in her sensorial heaviness, I could, by tolerat-ing the associated feelings, facilitate her own process of distin-guishing feelings (flow) and sensations (weight).

> She unfolds the blanket and places it carefully, lying down on her back. She makes soft movements with her hands and seems aware of gently breathing. I am aware of feelings of depression. She rolls away from me and back towards me. I ask about her feeling or thought here. She says her hands feel like tentacles and her middle is dark and contracting. She feels her hands are related to that. She curls away from me and stays there. I realize she is not in contact with me, nor I with her. I expe-rience a sad heaviness. She says she can just stay here in this stillness.

Her image of an underwater creature with tentacles reaching out and yet contracting away at the same time, not quite able to either latch on or to let go seemed to reflect something significant which she had said about her own infancy—breast feeding became impossible very early on, apparently because Beth suffered from bronchitis as an infant. (It is difficult to know precisely why this would necessitate premature weaning, but Beth seemed certain it had been the case.) Assuming it was so, then although the "pre-conception" of the breast, as Bion described it, may have been met initially—that is, the breast was there to relieve Beth's distress after birth, giving her the illusion of "creating" it—because the weaning (or dis-illusionment) had been premature, a psychophysically inte-grated state may not have had time to develop. Separation, in this case, would be all the more difficult to bear.[1]

## Bodily symptoms

Beth's unconscious psychic pain sometimes got translated into vari-ous bodily symptoms during the course of movement therapy. One of the most prominent of these was painful mouth ulcers, which twice appeared, uncannily, upon returning from visiting her parents in the North of England. There was a palpable feeling of deep despair.

> "I cannot speak or eat properly. I don't know whether to give up or to stay with it." I noticed myself feeling particularly bleak. I asked what it would mean to stay with it. "To stay alert," she responded, and then said, "I feel sad." She is lying on the floor. As she curls right into herself, my sensations give rise to an image of a lonely baby who does-n't want to complain. She suddenly burst into movement, a kind of Russian-dance-like squatting walk. I feel giddy, as if yanked from my reverie. I thought her tolerance for her lonely, empty feelings had suddenly reached a limit and she had had to move away. She spoke of the difficulty in breast-feeding (for the first time in therapy). After this session I felt drained, nauseous and bereft.

There were other bodily symptoms, but the mouth ulcers, in particular, seemed to stand for and replicate what may have been the original inaccessible, inexpressible feelings about the events of her infancy. The symptom, a symbolic equation, was doing the complaining for her. Over time it was gradually possible to tolerate a thinking space in which bodily symptoms could be experienced as symbolic communications; in which physical pain stood in for psychic pain.

## Unintegration

Beth's repeated need in this phase of therapy to share a passive state could be thought of as an attempt to replicate what Winnicott called unintegration, a re-creation of the total dependency of infancy or even of intra-uterine space. Unintegration brought forward into later life was described as a "developmental necessity" (Phillips, 1988, p. 80).

We can recognize the value of unintegration in supporting the opportunity to repattern inhibitory neuro-muscular patterns established in earliest life (recalling Bick's "second skin formations"). Patterns that resulted in physical symptoms and dissociated repetitions have a chance to alter, so that the musculature can release, breath, blood, and energy can flow more freely, and thoughts can become "thinkable". As feelings became more bearable for Beth, there was a growing recognition of the containment provided by therapy and a growing identification with a good container. This provided the grounding for a need to move on in time and space.

## Relationship to time

A dynamic relationship to time often seemed absent in these early sessions. When there are feeding difficulties, the "rhythm of safety"—a phrase used by Frances Tustin to describe an active interchange between mother and baby (Tustin, 1990)—can be disrupted. The mouth, in initiating grasping, sucking, releasing, reaching, measuring, has a primary role in developing this intersubjective rhythm. "Mouthing", as described in Body–Mind Centering, underlies and stimulates a relationship to space as well as time, through its reverberation through the spine (Hartley, 1989).

Sabbadini writes that ". . . the emergence of a sense of time would represent a bridge in the process of transformation from the temporally undifferentiated original world to the 'real' world of becoming, movement and change . . ." (Sabbadini, 1989, p. 478). Beth preferred to feel in control of an omnipresent time that does not move on for either herself or her object; this was often palpable in the countertransference. The ongoing steady rhythms of the breathing and the heartbeat, which *underlie* a more dynamic and conscious relationship with time, predominated. I associate this sense of timelessness with "body time"—it has more to do with "being" than with "doing" and is not responsive to time's ongo-ingness.

Laban links an active relationship to time with intuition. It was a year before Beth's intuitive impulses toward rhythmic aliveness were to resurface. A frustration started to set in; the shared space became claustrophobic. Having made contact with her affective body, her subsequent rhythmic revival, so to speak, was much more fully coloured with feeling. On several occasions there were inti-mations of a growing need to move away, as, at around nine months' of working together:

> She lies lethargically on the floor. Very suddenly she pushes against the floor. She says, "I want to get out of it. I feel closed in, I need to come up for air . . . but I can't . . . or I won't."

## Entering transitional space

Beth seemed to enter the space–time continuum with trepidation, often commenting that "I don't know what to do" or "I don't know where I'm going." Although there seemed to be an accumulation of felt experience and a growing impulse to move with it, she was reluctant to venture forth into "the big wide world". I often wondered if, at these times, she was overly concerned about the damage her underlying feelings might inflict on me. She managed the transition by making use of the folded blanket that was provided for her to sit on. It seemed like a classic transitional object (Winnicott, 1971). A cycle of exploration began which was a strong feature of the work for about three months.

> She moves her legs towards and away from her seat on the rug. I sense her "itchy feet". She shifts to a crouch, holding the rug, passing it from hand to hand, sliding it away on the floor, then pulling it back and through her legs. Then she goes crawling into the space. She laughs and says she feels support back there, pointing over her shoulder.

A few weeks later:

She stands, stamping and swivelling her feet, reaching down to stretch her whole body. She stands again and kicks the blanket round the room. She leaves it behind and pauses. When I enquire into the movement so far, she says she does not know what to do or where she is going. She only recognizes stiff shoulders. She comes to a crouch, places her hands softly on the floor, eyes closed. She folds into the floor, tenderly touching it with her lips. She says she feels shy and wants to hide in the blanket.

A month later:

She kneels on the rug and slides it with her as she crawls it forward under her knees. She seems to be very proud of doing this; there is a sprightly wagging movement in her very active spine. She leaves the rug after a bit and goes on crawling without it. She pauses extending her right leg back along the floor. She notes this is a familiar position from which she finds it hard to shift.

In these sequences, Beth was exploring how to sustain her inner experience as she moved "away" into the space, the delicate work of sustaining a sense of separateness without her internal space collapsing. Making her feelings manifest through active movement was a big step; the rug was felt to provide safety for both of us, I thought. By using the blanket, Beth moved on from the illusion of omnipotent control of the object, to an illusion of control by manipulation (Winnicott, 1971, p. 10).

It is noticeable in each of these three excerpts from clinical material that there is a point at which Beth's enthusiasm for the blanket's enabling power seems to fade away, leaving her feeling stuck or lost. I wondered if this represented the limitation of the internal object at this stage, the point at which the object became persecutory or "went dead". Perhaps Beth came up against her suspicions that her internal object had been seriously damaged by her earliest aggression, and this stopped her from risking going on, and possibly doing further damage.[2]

Because of Beth's high degree of sensory awareness, one could speculate that mother was indeed able to give her a sense of *physical* holding (Laban's weight); but perhaps she was unable to supply emotional or mental holding (Laban's flow or space) during the premature weaning process. My sense, based on my experience in the countertransference, was that they shared a rather lifeless and depressed state, one in which thinking was not possible.

As Beth increasingly trusted the therapeutic space, and dared to discover that moving away might lead somewhere interesting, the rug was relinquished as a transitional object. Winnicott quotes a patient who said of a transitional object: ". . . [it] might be very comfortable, but reality is more important than comfort" (*ibid.*, p. 30). What seemed to arise and crystallize in the next phase, as Beth began to take the space and express herself, was a striking and robust "spontaneous gesture".

## A particular "spontaneous gesture"

Winnicott wrote, "The spontaneous gesture is rooted in the body", and ". . . is the true self in action" (1960, p. 147). As gesture forms the basis of movement vocabulary, reading or receiving gesture is at the very heart of the movement psychotherapy process. In Beth's case, a recurring strong and deliberate clawing of fingernails on the floor betraying dark undercurrents of feeling that she had not previously allowed in seemed to give expression to a particularly spontaneous impulse. Other gestures, however smooth and clear, had not embodied this quality of aliveness. Beth seemed to be starting to feel that I might be resilient enough to tolerate her expression of feelings, and that separation might, indeed, be possible.

The scratching seemed to express a phantasy of invading and attacking. If, as hypothesized, Beth's disillusionment because of the loss of the breast, and the closeness with mother that it represented, was excessively abrupt, it is quite likely that feelings of this kind may have been present. But it is made more complicated by considering that the attacking nails may have also represented one view of the power of an *internal* object to hold Beth captive.

Beth's previous sense of merging with me may have been a way of avoiding feelings of being imprisoned claustrophobically inside mother as punishment for her phantasized attacks. This raises a question about the "spontaneous gesture" being simply an expression of the True Self. If the gesture represents the object inside the person, who does the gesture belong to? It would seem that traces of the object might always be expected to exist within the subject's spontaneous gestures. I would like to consider this in relation to the following.

> She stretches forward from sitting to crawling. Straight away her nails start to claw the floor as she crawls into the space. She laughs, saying she could scratch my floor but doesn't want to. I note her fear of doing damage. I say I imagine some part of her would like very much to scratch me as well as my floor, to get right inside. She agrees. Her breathing intensifies as she goes on. She comes to crouching. She says she feels like a leopard, scratching skin. I say it seemed to express quite primitive feelings (as these come across palpably). She starts pounding fists on floor. Then she stops and follows her index finger pressing along the floor. She said she felt she hadn't made any impact.

The picture presented is of an object that, it is felt, needed to be ripped open in this sadistic and primitive way; but even as she tried to claw her way in, there was a feeling of making no impact. This did seem to replicate some of the frustration and rage Beth may have experienced around feeding problems in infancy, which were being recreated in the transference.

Only after we both articulated in words the animal-like passion the movement betrayed, did Beth freely articulate these feelings, by pounding the floor. The powerful, primitive feelings expressed here, *passion drive* in Laban terms (including the elements of time, weight, and flow all at once) took her over for these moments— without attention to space, no part of her was available to monitor or control her feelings.

The energy was, however, quickly bound up and re-focused in space, as one finger alone scratched along its very deliberate path. This movement created the intensity of *spell drive*—strong weight, direct focus in space, and bound flow—but far from giving her a sense of spellbinding power, it left Beth with the feeling that she was not making any impact. Perhaps she was identifying with an internalized figure felt to be unable to make an impact in supporting the needy child emotionally. It recreated the sense of timelessness described in earlier sessions, but here, because of Beth's clarity of direction, I did not feel we shared a merged space.

In another excerpt, at 2½ years into the work, Beth was concerned that her feelings of rage were less easily controllable, and were spilling out into her relationship with her partner:

. . . She describes having felt a "tightness and clenching, like gritting teeth". I ask if she feels this now. She says no. Yet I have the feeling I am holding back her rage. She rather suddenly moves from sitting to crawling across the room; circling back, she begins to use her fingers like claws, lightly scratching the floor. She goes on with this and begins to cry. She keeps going and bursts into uncontrollable sobbing for a moment before gathering herself, stopping in a crawl stance. I ask what this sequence of movement had felt like. "Very, very angry," she said. I said I was struck by the relative lightness in her fingers, as if they seemed to convey something else as well. She said she didn't know why she started crying, then says, "I felt like a tiger tearing flesh." "Murderous feelings," I say. "Yes," she agrees, "murderous." I asked what she felt now, wondering about the after-effect. She said, "What did I do? What have I done?"

This is another example of how movement provides a way of gaining access and giving form to primitive, ambivalent feelings. I hope it provides the reader with a sense of the potential transformative power of attending to bodily as well as mental experience in psychotherapy settings.

Laban's *near state* (weight and time) described the quality I had seen in Beth when I first encountered her in the movement group. This movement was similar, but here the surge of physicality and impulse in time was integrated with her feelings. Her tears conveyed both a sense of relief in releasing the anger through this surge of liveliness, and the painful frustration associated with having kept feelings underground for so long. The conflict expressed in the fingers, the mixture of destructiveness and careful sensitivity, reflected the kinds of feelings Klein described as "depressive", in which the object is experienced as whole rather than split in two; and remorse can then be felt for phantasized attacks.

## The step by step journey to standing

In Beth's journey towards  separation, her movement vocabulary unfolded along a broadly developmental line, progressing from rolling and crawling to using the floor to press against in creeping on feet and hands, until she could gradually feel secure enough to come to standing and experience support from and relationship to the space. At times, when venturing into space, it felt as if an invisible umbilical cord connecting us was being stretched or ripped, and a visceral experience of loss was present in the countertransference. I felt myself to be experienced as a mother who could not survive on my own, which often carried a countertransference feeling of being physically weak compared to Beth.

The point of transition into movement was examined closely in terms of conflicting feelings stirred in Beth—the wish to stay forever in a timeless inside space alternated with the fear of being overwhelmed by a claustrophobic object, the wish not to initiate separation prematurely and risk abandonment, and the fear that potentially overwhelming feelings would erupt, including both rage and depressive concern for my welfare. There was marked ambivalence and uncertainty about where such an exploration would lead and what kind of containment I would be capable of providing. Because ambivalent feelings are given form in the present in movement psychotherapy, they are, I am suggesting, made more tangible and live than may be possible using words alone.

Around two years into the work, when these feelings were being explored,

> Beth looks at her feet; her toes seem alive and wiggly. She laughs saying she has baby feet, that people always told her she had feet like a toddler. She says they don't fit with her body. Is she saying she feels like a toddler, just learning to stand alone? She slides her feet vigorously on the floor.

Despite her initial ambivalence, Beth decided to risk discovering that both of us could tolerate and rejoice in her aliveness. She seemed able to explore the fact that her seemingly unused "baby feet", which had perhaps not had much of a feeling of security in contact with mother Earth, could begin to trust and enjoy making use of the relationship. This opened the way, in time, for her powerful and aggressive feelings to feel safe enough to stand with and embody. In a Labanian view, Beth was growing increasingly Effortfull. The dream state atmosphere, when enmeshed, gained momentum in time and finally focus in space, often without sacrificing the innate physical sensing of weight or the newly differentiated flow of feelings.

A sense of whole body commitment developed, as she began to feel that she could in fact make an impact on the object without fearing danger or retaliation. With this new impetus came a decision to do further professional training to develop her career and take steps to deepen her commitment to her long term partner. In our last year of working, Beth could increasingly express and embody her angry, aggressive feelings. There was noisy stamping and arm movements which sometimes reminded Beth of a boxer punching, or there were wild swinging movements, well supported by her strong lower body. She called these "lashing out".

On occasions when Beth freely expressed these feelings, I felt very enlivened by the effect of her vigorous movement. She was decidedly not trying to get rid of these feelings by putting them inside me; rather, she was communicating them in order to share them with me. She could, finally, freely put her strong and embodied feelings into the space in my presence. The journey seemed to reflect her having internalized the work of therapy, to stand on her own in relation to the world.

## Notes

1.  Daws emphasizes the crucial role the father makes in mitigating the effects of weaning. She makes the point that if father is "marginalized, felt to get in the way of an idealized mother–baby duo, then weaning might seem to be a disaster" (Daws, 1997). Although I have not discussed father's role in this family, Daws' thoughts seemed to be relevant.

2.  Alvarez points out that when transitional objects "slide over into becoming all-important, just as good as—or better than—the real human mother, enabling the child to ignore permanently and chronically this mother and the need for a living human being, they become symbolic equations or autistic objects" (Alvarez, 1992, p. 44). This did not happen with Beth.

# CHAPTER ELEVEN

# Signals from the solar plexus

"A traumatic event changes those who suffer it, and all change involves loss. . . . The question, however, is whether in the end the survivor will be less of a person than before, . . . or whether she can become more of a person, the disaster becoming a focus for growth"

(Garland, 1998, p. 6)

I sabel, a young Latin American woman, was a professional dancer whose career ended abruptly when she was badly injured in a motorway crash while on tour. Her best male friend and fellow dancer, the driver, died in the accident. At the suggestion of colleagues, Isabel came for movement psychotherapy three years later, after a lengthy recovery, when she was starting to rebuild her life. Initially, it seemed that she was only going through the motions of finding help.

Over the two and half years of weekly work, however, she seemed to rediscover the same inner tenacity that had motivated her to "choose life", as she vividly recalled feeling she had done when she lay terribly injured "in a space between life and death".

This psychophysical space was to be explored in some detail during the course of therapy. As she began to come to terms with the accident, Isabel was able to unravel some of the unconscious patterns and internal object relations that seemed to lie meaningfully beneath the surface.

Isabel had spent many months recovering in a hospital far from her home, quite unable to move and totally dependent on others for everything. She remembered this as a horrible time; she was unable to communicate except by blinking her eyes. The pain, fear and guilt she experienced during those months (and afterwards) often conspired to pull her toward a strong identification with her dead friend. Yet, through a powerful exertion of will by a part of herself, she was gradually able to recover the full use of her body, astonishing the doctors; though her whole left side, having taken the impact, was left quite weakened, and with some permanent damage.

Almost from the outset, Isabel found that in order to keep a sense of equilibrium in therapy, she preferred moving to talking—which, in the first phase, often meant performing familiar dance movements. At these times I usually felt my role to be that of an admiring audience. I was indeed drawn to the beauty of the movement, but its formality seemed, at times, to betray an emptiness of feeling. I felt that Isabel's movement during this period depicted the quality of dissociation known to be a natural response to trauma. Schore explained that following an initial state of hyper arousal, there is a withdrawal of feeling to create "an escape when there is no escape" (Schore, 2001a).

In these early sessions, I felt that if I did not intervene periodically to inquire about Isabel's thoughts, feelings, or sensations as she moved, we might spend entire sessions in this rather sterile performer–audience relationship. I felt as if I was experienced as an object with little to offer, who needed to be entertained by feats requiring technical precision such as turns and sustained arabesques. I often felt it was she, not me, who was the professional.

There was a sense in which I was needed to hold the overwhelming feelings of vulnerability and damage, while at the same time, to uncomfortably witness the bidding of a strict internal object as it imposed stringent physical demands. What the right side could do, the injured left side was expected to do equally well. Tests of balance were commonplace. There seemed to be some confusion in Isabel's mind about whether her intention in setting up these challenging tasks was to help herself overcome her injuries or to deny their existence.

There was a striving for an ethereal "upness", through rising to tiptoe, arching the upper back and reaching skywards, and a great reluctance to move "floorwards". At times the movements away from gravity and relationship with something supportive seemed to provide a retreat for Isabel from deep anxieties about dependency and especially the primitive feelings that had been re-stimulated by her experience in hospital.

Isabel seemed to be cut off from any experience of affect. In Laban's terms, although the movements were often smooth and fluid, they appeared, oddly, to lack the element of flow (of *feeling*). They could be described as "gliding"—Laban's term for a particular combination within the "action drive" (see Chapter Two) of light weight, direct space, and sustained time, or "floating"—light weight, sustained time, and flexible focus in space. These actions, which require intense concentration and focus of energy because motivated by harnessing time, weight, and space all at once, seemed to provide an alternative to, and protection from, coming into contact with powerful feelings associated with the trauma of the accident, and following that, the second trauma of such a long period of recovery. It was as if she wanted to protect us both from becoming submerged in this terrain.

*Perhaps the reader can sense in yourself the movement qualities that make up "floating" and "gliding", to recognize their protective way of maintaining equilibrium for Isabel.*

As Garland notes, trauma can elicit links with the "non-verbal or pre-verbal registers of experience", evoking primitive fears and phantasies. "It is this connection of past with present that is part of what makes the after-effects of trauma so hard to undo" (Garland, 1998, p. 13). As Isabel's feelings about dependency made their way into the transference, it became clear their origin long preceded the accident. In addition to coming to terms with the horrors of her recent trauma, part of the work would be to restore links to her own early bodily felt experience, and find words to think about and describe it.

*In between up and down*

The theme of moving up or down was often explored. I thought she was striving to find a place between the extremes, a safe middle ground between heaven and earth. In the twenty-first session:

> Standing, she leans forward, saying she wants to go down but cannot. She feels she will be hurt. She explores leaning forward, then folds herself into crawling. She comes to stillness for some time. I noticed I felt quite young, like a little girl who felt she had to have an adult mind. I asked what she notices. She says she feels her body is small and her head is big. That she is too small for her head. She lies on her back. Legs extend upward and move in the space. Here she feels better, though still considers it "in between up and down". She says she feels she's hiding something. It feels frustrating.

It seemed that strong anxieties were being hidden behind a façade of "normality", and lying down risked bringing the inner terrors to the surface. Isabel's tolerance for lying down was short at first. Yet she persisted in exploring this theme within therapy. Her vivid and painful association in the session was to the "one minute" during which she and her friend were both alive after the accident—that "it was both an eternity and nothing".

Lying down became an important element in Isabel's movement vocabulary, as she gradually increased her ability to tolerate the embodiment of her feelings (flow), and to make associations to her affective experience. Disturbing images arose when lying down, of crucifixion and drowning, and a memory surfaced of finding mother, having fainted, lying on the floor, and being taken for dead by Isabel as a young girl. These images held clues to very early persecutory phantasies. The precariousness associated with lying down was counterbalanced, so to speak, by the safer, more lyrical, and dancerly upward movements.

A most poignant and elemental example of the exploration of the "movement between up and down" occurred near the end of the therapy:

> she is moved to tears as she slowly and deliberately shifts her weight from the right leg to the damaged left leg as she simply stands in the space. She notes the feeling of going down into the left leg and going

up into the right. She realizes what depression she feels in going down, how it is associated with death and mourning, and how much she has wished to avoid this.

This was an example of the integration of painful psychophysical experience being clearly embodied in a simple but profound movement, which could be said to speak louder than words.

## Death as ever-present

Isabel felt convinced from earliest childhood that she was destined to be a dancer; she felt her parents had "expected a ballerina" even before she was born. Despite suffering various injuries throughout her career, oddly always to the left side of her body, she soldiered on under the impression that the emotional welfare of the family depended on it.

Describing the work of Frances Tustin, Mitrani writes,

> [Tustin] identified a pattern wherein babies who are born highly sensitive and intelligent, and with a great lust for life and beauty, are often overwhelmed with depressive anxiety when their preconception of a lively, responsive and caring object fails to materialize. While holding themselves responsible for this disturbance in the mother, they attempt to protect her omnipotently. [Mitrani, 2001, p. 36]

This statement helped me think about Isabel, as what also stood out was her use of omnipotent, narcissistic mechanisms of coping with her primitive fears by denying her need for help. The effect of this was strongly experienced in the countertransference—I felt in Isabel a precocious preoccupation with taking care of me, and an abiding lack of faith in my ability to help.

During the course of therapy, several real and imagined brushes with death came into focus. Isabel spoke of a certainty that she was fated to die before the age of twenty-one, perhaps suggesting Oedipal fears about the consequences of becoming an adult. And there were several instances during therapy when she feared being attacked on the street or hit by a car. These images presented a picture of an ever-present, life-threatening danger lurking in

Isabel's mind, and a lack of sustaining internal or external objects able to contain persecutory and envious feelings.

The car accident, it emerged, happened when Isabel's friend was very weary and a little drunk. She felt unable to stop him or to object to going along on what was felt to be a perilous journey. Unable to respond to her own sense of vulnerability and risk, she chose to bolster the confidence of her friend. She remembered distinctly being unable to think. As she recognized her persona, how she split off her own needs and doubts and located them in her friend, she felt increasing pain and isolation.

## Signals from the solar plexus

Isabel's infantile feelings, perhaps partly standing for a damaged internal object, seemed to be located in and identified with the middle of her body—the solar plexus—which, fittingly, could be said to be "in between up and down". It is a characteristic place for strong feelings—the proverbial "butterflies" and "gut reactions". Isabel's attitude toward the part of herself represented there softened over the course of therapy, as did the musculature. This enabled difficult feelings to flow through, so that psychophysical integration could begin to develop. The following are some excerpts from session notes describing her felt experience and associations to the solar plexus over time.

In the second session, when there were audible rumbling sounds from her tummy, Isabel

> responded by giving herself a swift punch in the solar plexus, in order to silence this spontaneous, unwelcome cry.

Embarrassed by her intolerant overreaction, she later in the session

> . . . held herself round the solar plexus and said she felt something heavy there, something brand new and needing protection. She then quickly opened her arms wide and arched her torso, projecting this vulnerable solar plexus to the ceiling. I thought this was an extreme change and I wondered if the strong willed performer part of herself had re-established its prominence.

By the fifth session, the intolerant approach had begun to give way to an attitude of curiosity about this part of her body that she knew held many painful feelings.

> She stood and holding her solar plexus, began to rotate and sway and turn, saying she was unwinding the solar plexus, which had felt tense. She went on and on arcing and looping, saying it was loosening.

The opening of the Pandora's Box of the solar plexus took its own time. To begin to recognize the issues that were keeping things "compacted", to use Isabel's word, took several months. The ability to unpack the parts of herself that had been split off and held tightly in the body, to enter into relationship with them—including parts that held the deep sadness and the savagery towards both self and internal objects—took courage as well as time.

In the fifty-sixth session,

> she describes feeling a heavy ball here, hand on solar plexus. I sense she is holding on to feelings, hiding something. She hints that I am mixed up with her bad feelings, perhaps am causing her to feel bad. She says when she leaves here she thinks that I'll be "keeping my distance" when she comes next time; but finds that I am not. So, she says, she is slowly learning it is okay to be herself here.

She seems to be expecting me to correspond to an internal container that is too slack, but finds that in reality I am firm enough to contain her. She allows her feelings to come forth. In a particularly moving segment round this time:

> She comes to stand but is hunched forward; she seems to be really feeling her solar plexus area, and her heartfelt feelings. Her arms seem to be directing energy diagonally forward and down. She remains still. I ask how it feels. "Bad," she says. I ask her to elaborate. "Just bad", is all she can muster. I feel a heavy-hearted sadness.

By the seventy-fifth session she had more words for describing her experience:

> . . . a block of ice, holding sadness. Old sadness. . . . She speaks of wanting to clean the space inside and makes vigorous hand movements. She has an image of fire.

She has begun to trust me enough to be able, at times, to feel that her aliveness will not stir up the depressed feelings in me which she felt herself to be the custodian of for an internalized depressed mother. She can stay with her real, fiery feelings, and thus they are intensifying.

She is absorbed by the feelings in the solar plexus in the seventy-eighth session.

> She sits and says she feels she exists inside this part of her body and nowhere else. She notes she used, in the first sessions, to feel she had to protect it. Now it's not needing protecting, but she feels she may never have inhabited her whole body. She touches her solar plexus, closes her eyes and begins to draw lines from there out into the space. After some time of this she tells me she doesn't know if she should go on. She is shocked by the image of snakes all tangled up inside, which she finds disgusting. She curves forward then lies on her back, as if she needs to give way to this feeling of being filled up.

> She says after a while there were also shouting human heads, but, "it's like watching TV; I am disengaged". She turns on to her side, facing me. I feel a wholeness in her presence and say that this doesn't seem so disengaged. She agrees, but says it is as if all this is going on inside and she cannot do anything. She sits. She makes a link to the accident, but says these feelings long precede the accident.

She seems to be describing a process of having long ago intro-jected these objects; she is partly addressing normal primitive Oedipal feelings—the difficulty of being on the outside of a couple who could not be brought together. Yet, it seems as if this couple has become trapped inside her, rather than being digested and moved through. The figures seem to reside there in the solar plexus in a quasi-concrete way.

## Splitting in the internal world

Melanie Klein described a state of internal reality in which the infant's impulses of love and hate are split, as to feel both for one and the same mother would be too anxiety-provoking for the baby. Its destructive impulses are aimed at a part object felt to be "bad", while its loving impulses are aimed at an (idealized) part object felt to be "good". The projection of "bad" qualities into an outer and, unconsciously, an internal, other gives rise to feelings of paranoia— threatening objects are felt to be liable to attack. In this process certain aspects of the self are disowned and projected outwards and/or lodged in tissues of the body.

The bodily splitting between "up and down" and also between left and right seemed, as well as being the obvious repercussions of the traumas of the recent past, to represent Isabel's attempts to maintain a primitive view of internal and external reality—right was good, left was bad, up was good, down was bad. As Isabel experienced these manifestations of splitting again and again in therapy, while also beginning to use me as someone who was able to receive her frightening, painful projections, things gradually began to be less rigidly divided on both physical and emotional levels. Embodied attentiveness created space for the split parts to be recognized, thought about, and joined up, and for internal reality to be distinguished from external.

As a key part of this process, Isabel could recall and recount details about the accident. These came out in small doses over the course of therapy, as if she wanted to spare both of us the pain and horror of taking in too much at once. Through her own creative work in therapy, the narcissistic state that she had initially clung to in order to shut off painful feelings, was slowly being relinquished, as depressive feelings and true mourning—not only for the terrible trauma of the accident, but also for the damage done through denying of internal objects and parts of herself—was allowed.

Isabel showed much courage in her overriding decision not to close off from long-held painful feelings, even if there was a "dance" of advancing and retreating. Symington writes quite passionately,

> In an analysis that aims at a cure of soul, a repetition of the original trauma arises again and again, and the individual has the opportunity to go down a different path. To choose the high ground includes excruciating pain. [Symington, 1994, p. 125]

## The dark lake

The seventieth session (six months before ending), provided long dreamlike movement sequences with very vivid associations. I felt the session heralded a significant ability for Isabel to recover her projections, receive her whole body's experience, and witness her own patterns.

Lying on her back, she reaches arms and legs softly upward. I feel a poignancy, a baby reaching up. I ask after a while for her thoughts . . . As in a dream, she speaks: "water . . ." . . . "grief . . ." . . . "very lonely . . ." She begins to slowly move all four limbs, bending at knees and elbows, eyes closed throughout. She continues, "a lake that is very old . . . undisturbed for a long time . . . very little life . . ." She says she is in it but she can breathe . . . she is a visitor. I sense she can enter and breathe in "the lake of grief", but can't quite feel she belongs. She says it is ghostly, like a cemetery.

She speaks of feeling cold. She holds her solar plexus and says that something is flowing. That it is cold but flowing. I say when something thaws out, it feels cold. She says she is aware of wanting to recapture her childhood; feels she ran through it, that time goes so fast.

She puts a hand on her solar plexus, initiating a long period of subtle movement. I feel fear in my own solar plexus, unsure if the feelings are mine or Isabel's. She stops to say she has been moving from her heart; that she always thought she moved from there; but it was really from here, pointing to her head. There are a few tears. She goes on. She says she's reminded of the time she tried to walk after the accident, and her foot gave way. She says this feeling is very old, not just from the accident.

In these sequences, she seemed to be inhabiting a very young and vulnerable place, while, at the same time processing the more recent trauma. Letting herself feel unboundaried seemed to mean letting go so that body, thoughts, and feelings can freely link up, while feeling, for the most part, safely contained.

It was difficult for Isabel to accept this intermingling of ambivalent feelings containing a mixture of love and hate, loss, envy and guilt, and impulses towards both life and death; but it seemed that she had internalized a strong enough good object, so that she could awaken the frightening parts of herself and reclaim them. A united couple was beginning to be found in her inner phantasy life, which allowed her to breathe out, to lie down, and bear witness. The real work of mourning was taking place.

Near the end of our work together, when Isabel was to return to Latin America, she spoke of her frozen feelings melting and flowing. As a dancer, she was acquainted with and used the Laban vocabulary herself; she told me that she could see that she confused bound flow with strong weight. What she perceived as a "show of strength" was actually a way of keeping herself from being overwhelmed by her feelings, and by death. This could be recognized by us both as a valuable and life-saving protection, one familiar since early childhood and now changing.

She felt she was learning what it is to play, and the notion of balance was something she no longer needed to rigidly impose on herself; rather it manifested in allowing ebbs and flows of feelings to move through her. The solar plexus, having started as a frozen place, and then become the location for grief, was felt in the end as a centre of strength. Having moved through many stages, Isabel could both speak about and embody her experience; she felt she was "entering a new world". She seemed intent on proceeding humbly and gracefully, one step at a time.

In this chapter I have described how movement functioned as a bridge to unify and balance body and psyche in working with the after-effects of trauma. Psychoanalytic thinking helped to reflect on Isabel's movement and to shed light on the meaning of bodily experience within the transference and countertransference. In my opinion, either perspective without the other may not have produced the same depth of work.

# Summary of Part III

"Knowledge is the product of split parts of the ego joining
up. The junction of parts comes about through action"

(Symington, 1994)

I
n writing the previous three chapters, I have drawn links
between psychoanalytic theory and movement analysis. There
are of course, many routes to Rome, as it were, but in this work
I feel it was the *synthesis* of the two processes that was instrumen-
tal in achieving the transformations described.

Each of the three patients worked to recognize the ways in
which they had placed obstacles in the way of psychophysical integration and embodiment of self. The working through of these
blocks, which manifested physically as well as mentally, was
accomplished through examining the patterns that came to light
within movement psychotherapy. The patterns were found to have
their deepest roots in body-based processes of early childhood or
infancy.

It could be speculated that in each case there was a weak internalized object, which had established a sense of helplessness very

early on in these patients' lives that interfered with normal child-hood dependence. "One's relationship with one's body initially stems from and corresponds to one's relationship with one's mother" (Judd, 2000). It seemed probable that the mothers of these women had to deal with major emotional difficulties of their own, which may have even been heightened by the birth of their daugh-ters. In their different ways, these patients felt the need to provide containment for themselves, and at times, for their internalized maternal objects as well, in a reversal of roles.

The split off parts showed up in the transference to me—I was felt to be variously untrustworthy, weak, intrusive, needing looking after, and the object of savage rage. When these projected aspects were able to be taken back inside themselves, there was a renewal of energy that, in each case, was expressed in their expansion of movement vocabulary. This led to a more embodied sense of self; and as the non-verbal channels were opened and the energy and breath flowed more freely, so words were found to make sense of feelings.

The patients' transformation from stuck patterns of relation-ships with both object and self to deeper and more fluid patterns of relating in which ambivalent feelings could be borne, have been broadly summed up in both movement and psychoanalytic terms. I have tried to provide a synthesis of the two perspectives by describing the movement dynamics (Effort qualities)—especially which ones were present or absent—and by thinking about which ones accounted for defences and which for integration.

Although it was impossible for elements of theory from both perspectives not to find their way into my mind from time to time during sessions, I did not usually consciously name these. The emotional impact of the relationships and the communication of feeling and psychic states through movement and stillness, silence and speech, the impact of the transference and the countertransfer-ence, was the absorbing focus.

Each patient can be said to have moved from a two-dimensional to a more three-dimensional way of relating to trauma and loss, in which a sense of perspective was achieved. In movement terms, these can be summarized as follows.

*Francine*'s innate strengths were a strong mind, imagination, and visual sense; she was strong in Laban's space Effort, showing both direct and flexible attention to the outside world. The horizontal plane, which has an affinity with attention to space, was her primary mode of orientation to the world. An acceleration in time— the impulse to take flight from feelings—was invoked as a characteristic response to anxiety. Time and space (decisions and thoughts)—the awake state, space and flow (thoughts and feelings)—the remote state, and time and flow (decisions and feelings)—the mobile state, were all easily accessible for her. The combination of all three of these elements—space, time, and flow were seen to motivate Francine altogether at times of heightened involvement with imagery and associations stimulated by her movement, creating Laban's weightless "vision drive".

States involving the physical sensing of weight were more challenging; and it was as if an embodied internal three-dimensionality was weak. Yet, through invoking her strong mind, she was increasingly successful in accessing weight, and with it a sense of physical presence and a relationship to gravity. Gradually she could let go of her attention to me and indulge in the inner focused sensory, dream state, the clear intent of near state, and the "chaos" of passion drive. This acquisition of a fuller range of possibilities depended on the healing of an internal object and a reappraisal of psychophysical attitudes deriving from childhood.

*Beth's* journey from two to three-dimensionality was almost directly opposite to that Francine's. She had taken refuge in a sensory world, dissociated from a flow of thoughts or feelings. This seemed to result from a premature period of weaning that had been difficult for both herself and her mother to negotiate and to mourn. Weight was her most prominent Effort quality, and her relationship to gravity in the vertical axis, as experienced from a passive lying down position, was the starting place from which she gradually entered the space-time continuum.

Beth had preferred to inhabit an internal world as if, in phantasy, she resided in a protected, albeit claustrophobic, inside space, at times seeming not yet born. Gradually it became possible for Beth to wake up to powerful feelings (flow) that needed to be expressed outwardly, not only held inside. The alertness engendered by waking up to the passage of time and making her own decisions, and to the mental awareness and thinking associated with attention to space, (both of which had previously been defended against), were incorporated into her vocabulary. With a fuller range of possibilities, I began to see moments of spell drive and passion drive as her preferred ways of embodying heightened feeling states. Though the former is timeless and the latter is spaceless, both include weight, Beth's strongest element. As Beth also gained the ability to reflect on her feelings and experience separation and the mourning associated with it, she, too, replaced childhood patterns with adult ones and had a much wider range of movement.

*Isabel* had a great sensitivity to time. Having gained a wisdom about mortality through tragic circumstances, she knew how to savour a moment. Yet, she could often not tolerate the reality of her physical and emotional state—Laban's dream state (weight and flow). Like Francine, she strived to present an alert and independent persona, as if trying to live up to someone else's image. Her defensive performed actions could be described in terms of Laban's near state (sustained time and light weight) or "action drive", including all the elements except flow (feelings). As she was able to yield to her feelings, and to me as a capable object, her internal world became fuller; and, as for Francine, the dream state became tolerable. Isabel could come down to earth, relinquish her elevated performer's stance, and begin to mobilize her innate talent and optimism in the service of her own adult hopes and desires.

## Links between adults and subjects of infant observation

Parallels can be drawn between the primitive defences or coping mechanisms used by the adults and defences used by the infants and young children described in Part Two.

Francine was seen to have had similar kinds of difficulties of intersubjectivity and attunement as baby Rodney, discussed in Chapter Six, whose mother had incurred a head injury as a result of a fall during her own infancy. Whereas Rodney used speed to flee from his affect-laden experience, Francine distanced herself through using her mind and imagination to latch on to images.

For both Beth and baby Sherry in Chapter Six, negotiating separation, initiating movement of their own, was fraught with difficulty.

And Isabel, in her omnipotent striving in the face of trauma, was reminiscent of Sam's story in Chapter Five; Sam strived in a manic way to display his "grown-upness" in the face of a frightening lack of control over his turbulent start in life.

All the women were successful in shifting their primitive infantile patterns, taking back projections and successfully transforming their internal worlds. The transformations were evident in both their embodied experience through movement and their psychological and emotional states. It can be conjectured, however, that their early patterns for coping with stress had not been changed forever; rather, they had been made conscious, and the recognition and management of them by the patients themselves in future would now be more possible.

In all three cases the inbuilt human impulses to shut off from pain and to take whatever steps are necessary in order not to feel the primitive terrors and grief at the core of one's being were painstakingly revealed. On the other side, thankfully, was the impulse to know truth.

# CHAPTER TWELVE

# Conclusions

"I am sure therapists need a model of non-verbal communication based upon acceptance of intrinsic affective states and
their communication"

(Trevarthen, 2004, p. 11)

*Recapping basic themes*

My aim in this book has been to bring movement analysis
and psychoanalysis into contact with one another, in
order to see whether and in what ways the two disciplines were mutually compatible and informative. This has been
explored in Part I by way of a comparison and synthesis of the theoretical frameworks of psychoanalytic object relations and movement analysis/movement therapy. In Part II, I brought both
disciplines to bear on the discussion of material from four psychoanalytic observational studies; and in Part III I presented material
from three patients in individual movement psychotherapy, in
which a blending of the two disciplines was described.

From my perspective as a movement psychotherapist, I started from the premises that body and mind are inseparable, and that the body is an important site of knowledge about self and relationship. I have described how paying attention to the body by both patient and therapist provides insights into primitive impulses. Awareness of the body and its movement has been shown to support the recognition, integration, and balancing of different realms of experience—physical, mental and emotional.

I have highlighted elements of psychoanalytic theory that explore and elucidate infantile object relations and their effect on development throughout the life cycle. And I have introduced LMA, a language useful for describing the non-verbal expression of object relations.

## Movement training for actors

I have also written about how this blending of the perspectives of movement analysis and psychoanalysis has provided a framework for my teaching of movement for actors. This exploration gets to the heart of what it means to embody psychological and emotional experiences, which is essential to the actor's art and training. The LMA vocabulary, enhanced by its conjunction with both Suryodarmo's non-stylized Amerta Movement practice and the links that have been drawn with psychoanalytic thinking, supports teachers of movement in being able to offer a safe space for actors' creativity to be released. The safe boundaries created by the movement analysis framework make it possible to methodically explore the unknown with abandon and to more fully and consciously embody the imagination.

## What psychoanalysis brings to movement analysis and DMT

Although LMA gives names to elements of movement that denote various states of mind, it does not offer a theoretical framework within which to think and speak about how and why specific movement qualities are used. The depth of understanding of psychological processes and object relations that psychoanalysis provides thus augments the significance of LMA concepts and categories as applied to DMT. Such concepts as splitting, projective identification, depressive functioning, etc. can greatly enrich the meaning of bodily felt experience.

Psychoanalytic thinking, by informing the intersubjective relationship between therapist and patient (and between patients in a group), provides a window through which insight into transference and countertransference processes in DMT may be made more conscious and available for thought. The psychoanalytic perspective, by providing words to mediate between physical sensations and turbulent feelings, makes it more possible to tolerate and reflect on experience.

There was not seen to be a direct correlation between specific movement qualities and specific psychic processes. The dream state for example, characterized a defence against separation used by Beth, yet for Isabel it marked a move towards integration. I think it is clear that the descriptions of complex psychological processes made possible by psychoanalysis is beyond the range of LMA and can further enhance much work in DMT. Conversely, LMA and Amerta describe a language of sensation and perception that may provide a valuable added resource for psychoanalysis.

## What movement analysis offers psychoanalysis

Many psychoanalysts have pointed to the importance of deepening their work with non-verbal experience, that level of communication which precedes or is beyond words (McDougall,1989, 1995; Milner, 1969; Pally, 2003; Quinodoz, 2003, etc.). I have suggested that LMA, by providing a vocabulary for detailed articulation (in movement and words) of experiential phenomena, provides a valuable framework and system of categories for bringing the interrelationships between body and psyche into greater focus.

As has been suggested, the experiential language of movement can play a central role in heightening the recognition and subtle discrimination of moment to moment changes within transference and countertransference processes; it can provide an avenue for therapists to "listen" to and define both their own and their patients' bodily felt experience.

Consciously or unconsciously, experience that evokes the patient's internal object relationships is transferred from patient to therapist. I have suggested that attention to the body and movement as part of therapy may add to therapists' ability to bring projective identification out into the open in a helpful way, allowing both parties to recognize in themselves the physical component of introjective and projective processes. In this way, projections that may have started out as defensive unconscious evacuations may begin to be seen to include adaptive sensoriaffective patterns of communication, as Bion has indicated (1962).

I have also suggested that LMA and movement experience may:

- provide an intermediate link between raw experience and thinking;
- be a guide for making psychoanalytic metaphors like "second skin" more tangible;
- provide a more direct avenue for including both patients' own bodily experience and therapists' somatic countertransferential experience in the work of any therapy.

The capacity to acknowledge and respond to felt experience, including where and how it is experienced in the body, is, I have suggested, an essential ingredient in the formation of new neuromuscular pathways and the embodiment of new mental perspectives. I have suggested that the process of free association can incorporate awareness not only of what is experienced in thought but also of what is experienced by *dwelling* (or not!) in the body.

### Synthesis of two frameworks

Bucci (1985) suggests that one task of psychoanalysis is "translation between the verbal and nonverbal representation systems". It seems that the frameworks for analysis I have brought into relationship with one another, which have been shown to provide separate but mutually informative perspectives on the same material, could support this task for both professions. I have suggested that in each field the perspective of the other is implied, but could be more fully elaborated.

Interdisciplinary approaches are increasingly recognized as helpful in addressing the primitive realm of infantile experience, with reference to both fundamental sensoriaffective experience and primary object relations as well as in exploring the enduring effects of both throughout the life cycle. I have referred to the growing body of fruitful work that involves cooperative exploration among disciplines such as psychoanalysis, neuroscience, child development, infant observation, attachment theory, and dance movement therapy. I have described my own practice in individual movement psychotherapy, informed by psychoanalytic theory and observational studies, which aims to synthesize two frameworks.

## Who benefits from this work?

In my opinion, this interdisciplinary blending of approaches has the potential for extending the work with patients in either movement psychotherapy/DMT or psychotherapy. But clearly those for whom the preverbal stage of development was the source of trauma or difficulty should be seen as primary candidates. I cannot help thinking that people who struggled or failed to achieve "good enough" object relationships in infancy could benefit from the use of embodied attentiveness and movement as part of therapy. Movement psychotherapy can foster a capacity to tolerate the residual effects of primitive frustrations and internal conflicts.

Also, adult or child patients for whom verbal and symbolic communication is difficult—those on the autistic spectrum, those with psychosomatic symptoms, those who dissociate from sensory stimuli, who were perhaps abused or neglected, children with ADD or other learning difficulties—are all potentially good candidates for a form of therapy based on a blending of the two frameworks I have described.

## Next steps towards developing these ideas

It is my hope that this book might provide a catalyst for promoting dialogue between psychoanalysts/psychotherapists and movement psychotherapists/DMTs, that it might encourage discussion and debate to draw out the areas of overlap, making them more explicit. Conferences, contributions to Continuous Professional Development (CPD) in both fields, as well as the writing of articles, will provide forums for getting the ball rolling. Eventually, I think that some adaptations in training could be considered, although both the practicalities of finding time for new components in training, and the inevitable challenges to professional identity that taking on new ideas might stir up, could militate against such changes.

As Orbach has said, it is in the process of giving form to experience that transformation occurs (2002). I have attempted in this book to describe a method that I believe facilitates such a process. I have suggested that for some (if not all) patients, enabling an experience of the physical depths within the therapeutic encounter can facilitate a sinking into the most painful, repressed and neglected layers of the infantile psyche; and that if this is made use of in the therapeutic relationship, it can in turn both enliven and integrate.

# REFERENCES

Adler, J. (2002). *Offering from the Conscious Body: The Discipline of Authentic Movement*. Rochester, VT: Inner Traditions.

Ainsworth, M. D. S., Blehar, M. C., Waters, E., & Wall, S. (1978). *Patterns of Attachment: A Psychological Study of the Strange Situation*. Hillsdale, NJ: Erlbaum.

Alvarez, A. (1992). *Live Company*. London: Routledge.

Alvarez, A. (1998). Form in unconscious phantasy, thinking and walking. Manuscript unpublished in English.

Alvarez, A., & Reid, S. (Eds.) (1999). *Autism and Personality: Findings from the Tavistock Autism Workshop*. London: Routledge.

Anzieu, D. (1989). *The Skin Ego*. New Haven, CT: Yale University Press.

Aposhyan, S. (1999). *Natural Intelligence: Body–Mind Integration and Human Development*. Baltimore, MD: Williams and Wilkins.

Bartenieff, I. (1980). *Body Movement: Coping with the Environment*, New York: Gordon and Breach.

Bateson, G. (1972). *Steps to an Ecology of the Mind*. New York: Ballantine.

Beebe, B., & Lachmann, F. M. (1988). Mother–infant mutual influence and precursors of psychic structure. In: A. Goldberg (Ed.), *Progress in Self Psychology* (Vol. 3, pp. 3–25). Hillsdale, NJ: Analytic Press.

Beebe, B., & Lachmann, F. M. (2002). *Infant Research and Adult Treatment: Co-constructing Interactions*. New York: Analytic Press.

Bick, E. (1968). The experience of the skin in early object relations. *International Journal of Psychoanalysis, 49*: 484–486.

Bick, E. (1986). Further considerations on the function of the skin in early object relations. *British Journal of Psychotherapy, 18*(1). Reprinted in: A. Briggs (Ed.), *Surviving Space: Papers on Infant Observation* (pp. 60–71). London: Karnac.

Bion, W. (1962). *Learning from Experience*. London: Heinemann.

Bion, W. (1963). *Elements of Psycho-Analysis*, London: Heinemann.

Bion, W. (1970). *Attention and Interpretation*. London: Tavistock.

Bloom, K. (1994). Movement as a medium for psychophysical integration. Unpublished MA thesis, Unversity of East London, Department of Psychosocial Studies.

Bollas, C. (1987). *The Shadow of the Object: Psychoanalysis of the Unthought Known*. London: Free Association.

Bollas, C. (1992). *Being a Character*. London: Routledge.

Bonnard, A. (1960). The primal significance of the tongue. *International Journal of Psycoanalysis, 40*: 301–307.

Bowlby, J. (1988). *A Secure Base*. London: Routledge.

Briggs, A. (Ed.) (2002). *Surviving Space: Papers on Infant Observation*. London: Karnac.

Britton, R. (1998). *Belief and Imagination*. London: Routledge.

Bucci, W. (1985). Dual coding: a cognitive model for psychoanalytic research. *Journal of the American Psychoanalytic Association, 33*: 571–607.

Carroll, R. (1997). Unpublished manuscript.

Carroll, R. (2002), Unpublished manuscript.

Charles, M. (2001). Nonphysical touch: modes of containment and communication within the analytic process. *Psychoanalytic Quarterly, LXX*: 387–416.

Chekhov, M. (2002). *To the Actor*. New York: Routledge.

Chodorow, J. (1991). *Dance Therapy and Depth Psychology*. London: Routledge.

Cohen, B. B. (1987). The action in perceiving. *Contact Quarterly*, Fall: 22–28.

Cohen, B. B. (1993). *Sensing, Feeling, and Action*, Northampton, MA: Contact Editions.

Damasio, A. (1994). *Descartes's Error*, London: Picador.

Damasio, A. (1999) *The Feeling of What Happens*, London: Heinemann.

Darwin, C. R. (1872). *The Expression of Emotions in Man and Animals*. London: John Murray.

Daws, D. (1997). The perils of intimacy: closeness and distance in feeding and weaning. *Journal of Child Psychotherapy*, 23(2): 179–197.

Dosamentes, E. (1990). Movement and psychodynamic pattern changes in long-term dance/movement therapy groups. *American Journal of Dance Therapy*, 12(1): 27–44.

Dyrud, J. (1993). Foreword. In: M. Chace, S. Sandel, S. Chaiklin, & A. Lohn (Eds.), *Foundations of Dance/Movement Therapy: The Life and Work of Marion Chace*. Washington, DC: American Dance Therapy Association.

Edwards, J. (2000). On being dropped and picked up: adopted children and their internal objects. *Journal of Child Psychotherapy*, 26(3): 349–367.

Edwards, J. (Ed.) (2001). *Being Alive: Building on the Work of Anne Alvarez*. E. Sussex: Routledge.

Fraiberg, S. (1982). Pathological defences in infancy. *Psychoanalytic Quarterly*, 51: 612–635.

Freeman, T. (1971). Observations on mania. *International Journal of Psychoanalysis*, 52: 479–486.

Freud, S. (1905d). Three essays on the theory of sexuality. *S.E.*, 7: 135–243. London: Hogarth.

Freud, S. (1905e). Fragment from an analysis of a case of hysteria. *S.E.*, 7: 7–122. London: Hogarth.

Freud, S. (1912e). Recommendations to physicians practising psychoanalysis. *S.E.*, 12: 111–120. London: Hogarth.

Freud, S. (1920g). Beyond the pleasure principle. *S.E.*, 18. London: Hogarth.

Freud, S. (1923b). The ego and the id. *S.E.*, 19: 13–27. London: Hogarth.

Garland, C. (1998). *Understanding Trauma*. London: Karnac.

Grotstein, J. (2001). Foreword. In: J. Mitrani, *Ordinary People and Extra-Ordinary Protections*. London: Routledge.

Haag, G. (1991). Some reflections on body ego development through psychotherapeutic work with an infant. In: R. Szur, and S. Miller (Eds.), *Psychoanalytic Psychotherapy with Children, Adolescents and Families* (pp. 135–145). London: Karnac.

Haag, G. (2000). In the footsteps of Frances Tustin: further reflections on the construction of the body ego. *International Journal of Infant Observation and Its Applications*, 3: 7–22.

Hagen, U. (1973). *Respect for Acting*. New York: Macmillan.

Hardy, B. (1975). *Tellers and Listeners: The Narrative Imagination*. London: Athlone.

Hartley, L. (1989). *The Wisdom of the Body Moving*. Berkeley, CA: North Atlantic Books.

Heimann, P. (1950). On counter-transference. *International Journal of Psycho-Analysis, 31*: 81–84.

Hinshelwood, R. D. (1989). *A Dictionary of Kleinian Thought*. London, Free Association.

Hinshelwood, R. D. (1994). *Clinical Klein*. London: Free Association.

Houzel, D. (2001). Bisexual qualities of the psychic envelope. In: J. Edwards (Ed.), *Being Alive: Building on the Work of Anne Alvarez* (pp. 44–56). E. Sussex: Routledge.

Isaacs, S. (1952). The nature and function of phantasy, In: M. Klein, P. Heimann, S. Isaacs, & J. Riviere (Eds.), *Developments in Psychoanalysis*. London: Hogarth, [reprinted London: Karnac, 1989].

Jacobs, T. J. (1994). Nonverbal communications: some reflections on their role in the psychoanalytic process and psychoanalytic education. *Journal of the American Psychological Association, 42*, 741–762.

Jackson, J., & Nowers, E. (2002). The skin in early object relations revisited. In: A. Briggs (Ed.), *Surviving Space: Papers on Infant Observation* (pp. 208–225). London: Karnac.

Joseph, B. (1959). An aspect of the repetition compulsion. In: E. B. Spillius & M. Feldman (Eds.), *Psychic Equilibrium and Psychic Change* (pp. 16–33). London: Routledge, 1989.

Joseph, B. (1981). Towards the experiencing of psychic pain. In: E. B. Spillius & M. Feldman (Eds.), *Psychic Equilibrium and Psychic Change* (pp. 88–97). London: Routledge, 1989.

Joseph, B. (1989). Psychic change and the psychoanalytic process. In: E. B. Spillius & M. Feldman (Eds.), *Psychic Equilibrium and Psychic Change* (pp. 192–202). London: Routledge.

Judd, D. (2000). The Never Land—loss of an idealized pre-birth place and the gain of a thinking mind. *Journal of Child Psychotherapy, 26*(2): 235–257.

Jung, C. G. (1921). *Psychological Types (Collected Works of C. G. Jung, Volume 6)* [reprinted London: Routledge & Kegan Paul, 1971].

Jung, C. G. (1961). Symbols and the interpretation of dreams. *CW, 18*: 185–200.

Kemp-Welch, A. (2001). Rituals of chaos: the movement work of Suprapto Suryodarmo, *Contemporary Theatre Review, 11*(2): 55–68.

Kestenberg Amighi, J., Loman, S., Lewis, P., & Sossin, M. K. (1999). *The Meaning of Movement*. Amsterdam: Gordon and Breach.

Klein, M. (1932). *The Psychoanalysis of Children*, London: Hogarth [reprinted London: Virago, 1989].

Klein, H. S. (1973). Emotion, time and space. *Bulletin of the British Psychoanalytical Society*, *68*: 1–9.

Klein, M. (1946). Notes on some schizoid mechanisms. In: *The Writings of Melanie Klein* vol. 3, *Envy and Gratitude and Other Works* (pp. 1–24). London: Hogarth.

Laban, R. (1950). *The Mastery of Movement*. London: MacDonald and Evans.

Laban, R. (1966). *The Language of Movement*, London: MacDonald and Evans.

La Barre, F. (2001). *On Moving and Being Moved*. New York: Analytic Press.

Lechavalier-Haim, B. (2001). From freezing to thawing: working toward the depressive position in long-term therapy with autistic patients. In: J. Edwards (Ed.), *Being Alive: Building on the Work of Anne Alvarez* (pp. 89–101). E. Sussex: Routledge.

Leuzinger-Bohleber, M., & Pfeifer, R. (2002). Remembering a depressive primary object: memory in the dialogue between psychoanalysis and cognitive science. *International Journal of Psychoanalysis*, *83*(Pt 1): 3–33.

Lewis, P. (1979). *Theoretical Approaches in Dance-Movement Therapy*, *Vol 1*. Dubuque, IA: Kendall/Hunt.

Likierman, M. (2001). *Melanie Klein: Her Work in Context*. London: Continuum.

Lynch, M. (2000). The role of the body as the medium in child psychotherapy: snapshots of therapy with an 11 year old, severely abused, multiply placed girl. *Journal of Child Psychotherapy*, *26*(2): 159–181.

Main, M., & Cassidy, J. (1988). Categories of response to reunion with the parent at age 6: Predictable from infant attachment classifications and stable over a 1-month period. *Developmental Psychology*, *24*, 415–426.

Maiello, S. (2000). Broken links: attack or breakdown? *Journal of Child Psychotherapy*, *26*(1): 5–24.

Maletic, V. (1987). *Body, Space, Expression*. Berlin: de Gruyter.

McDougall, J. (1986). *Theatres of the Mind*. London: Free Association.

McDougall, J. (1989). *Theatres of the Body*. London: Free Association.

McDougall, J. (1995). *The Many Faces of Eros*. London: Free Association.

Meloche, M. (1988). Body limits, time and space in psychosomatic organization. *Journal of the Melanie Klein Society*, *6*(1): 5–13.

Meltzer, D. (1960). Lectures and seminars in Kleinian child psychiatry (lectures given at the Tavistock Clinic in 1960). In: D. Hahn (Ed.),

*Sincerity and Other Works: Collected Papers of Donald Meltzer* (pp. 35–89). London: Karnac, 1994.

Meltzer, D. (1975a) Adhesive identification. *Contemporary Psycho-Analysis*, 11: 289–310.

Meltzer, D. (1975b). Dimensionality as a parameter of mental functioning: its relation to narcissistic organization. In: D. Meltzer, J. Bremner, S. Hoxter, D. Weddell, & I. Wittenberg (Eds.), *Explorations in Autism: A Psycho-Analytical Study* (pp. 223–238). Strathtay, Perthshire, Clunie Press.

Meltzer, D. (1981). The relation of splitting of attention to splitting of self and objects. In. D. Hahn (Ed.), *Sincerity and Other Works: Collected Papers of Donald Meltzer* (pp. 475–482). London: Karnac, 1994.

Merleau-Ponty, M. (1964). The child's relations with others. In: J. M. Edie (Ed.), *The Primacy of Perception* (pp. 96–155). Evanston, IL: Northwestern University Press.

Milner, M. (1950). *On Not Being Able to Paint*. London: Heinemann.

Milner, M. (1960). The concentration of the body. In: *The Suppresed Madness of Sane Men* (pp. 234–240). London: Tavistock, 1987.

Milner, M. (1969). *Hands of the Living God*. London: Hogarth [reprinted London: Virago, 1988].

Mitrani, J. (2001). *Ordinary People and Extra-Ordinary Protections*. London: Brunner-Routledge.

Mori, S. (2001). The role of the self-object experience in the therapy of an autistic child: from lying flat to launching a spaceship. *Journal of Child Psychotherapy*, 27(2): 159–173.

Moscowitz, M., Monk, C., Kaye, C., & Ellman, S. J. (Eds.) (1997). *The Neurobiological and Developmental Basis for Psychotherapeutic Intervention*. Northvale, NJ: Jason Aronson.

North, M. (1972). *Personality Assessment Through Movement*. London: Plays, Inc.

Ogden, T. (1997). *Reverie and Interpretation: Sensing Something Human*. Northvale, NJ: Jason Aronson; London: Karnac.

Ogden, T. (2001). *Conversations at the Frontier of Dreaming*, Northvale, NJ, Jason Aronson.

Orbach, S. (2002). The false self and the false body. In: B. Kahr (Ed.), *The Legacy of Winnicott* (pp. 124–134). London: Karnac.

Pallaro, P. (1996). Self and body-self: dance/movement therapy and the development of object relations. *The Arts in Psychotherapy*, 23(2): 113–119.

Pally, R. (2003). A primary role for nonverbal communication in psychoanalysis, *Psychoanalytic Inquiry*, 21(1): 71–92.

Panksepp, J. (1998). *Affective Neuroscience*. New York: Oxford University Press.

Parsons, M. (2000). *The Dove that Returns, the Dove that Vanishes*. London: Routledge.

Phillips, A. (1988). *Winnicott*. Cambridge, MA: Harvard University Press.

Pines, M. (1984). Mirroring in group analysis as a developmental and therapeutic process. In: T. E. Lear (Ed.), *Spheres of Group Analysis* (pp. 20–28). London: Leinster Leader.

Piontelli, A. (1992). Introduction and Chapter 1: Fetal behaviour and fetal environment. In: *From Fetus to Child* (pp. 1–38). London: Tavistock/Routledge.

Poynor, H. (1998). Women–body–movement. Unpublished MA thesis, University of Bristol, Department of Drama.

Quinodoz, D. (2003). *Words That Touch*. London: Karnac.

Resnik, S. (1995). *Mental Space*. London: Karnac.

Resnik, S. (1987). *The Theatre of the Dream*. London: Tavistock.

Resnik, S. (2001). *The Delusional Person: Bodily Feelings in Psychosis*. London: Karnac.

Rey, H. (1988). Schizoid phenomena in the borderline. In: E. B. Spillius (Ed.), *Melanie Klein Today: Mainly Theory* (pp. 203–229). London: Routledge.

Rey, H. (1994). *Universals of Psychoanalysis in the Treatment of Psychotic and Borderline States*. London: Free Association.

Rhode, M. (2002). Whom does the skin belong to? Trauma, communication, and a sense of self. In: A. Briggs (Ed.), *Surviving Space: Papers on Infant Observation* (pp. 226–239). London: Karnac.

Rosenfeld, D. (1992). *The Psychotic Aspects of the Personality*. London: Karnac.

Rustin, M. (1998). Observation, understanding and interpretation: the story of a supervision. *Journal of Child Psychotherapy*, 24(3): 433–448.

Rustin, M. (2001). The therapist with her back against the wall. *Journal of Child Psychotherapy*, 27(3): 273–284.

Rustin, M. (2002). Struggles in becoming a mother: Reflections from a clinical and observational standpoint. *Infant Observation*, 5(1): 7–20.

Rustin, M. J. (2002). Looking in the right place: complexity theory, psychoanalysis and infant observation. *International Journal of Infant Observation*, 5(1): 122–144.

Rustin, M. J. (2003). Research in the consulting room. *Journal of Child Psychotherapy, 29*: 137–145.

Sabbadini, A. (1989). How the infant develops a sense of time. *British Journal of Psychotherapy, 5*(4): 475–483.

Salo, F. T., Paul, C., Morgan, A., Jones, S., Jordan, B., Meehan, A., Morse, S., & Walker, A. (1999). Free to be playful. *International Journal of Infant Observation, 3*: 47–62.

Sandler, J. (1976). Countertransference and role-responsiveness. *International Journal of Psychoanalysis, 3*: 43–47.

Satyamurti, C. (2003). "First time ever": writing the poem in potential space. In: H. Canham and C. Satyamurti (Eds.), *Acquainted with the Night* (pp. 31–48). London: Karnac.

Scheler, M. (1913). *The Nature of Sympathy*. London: Routledge & Kegan Paul, 1954.

Schore, A. S. (1994). *Affect Regulation and the Origin of Self: The Neurobiology of Emotional Development*. Hillsdale, NJ: Lawrence Erlbaum.

Schore, A. S. (2001a). Neurobiology, developmental psychology, and psychoanalysis: convergent findings on the subject of projective identification. In: J. Edwards (Ed.), *Being Alive: Building on the Work of Anne Alvarez* (pp. 57–74). E. Sussex: Routledge.

Schore, A. S. (2001b). The effects of early relational trauma on right brain development, affect regulation and infant mental health. *Infant Mental Health Journal, 22*: 201–269.

Schore, A. S. (2002). Clinical implications of a psychoneurobiological model of projective identification. In: S. Alhanati (Ed.), *Primitive Mental States* (pp. 1–65), London: Karnac.

Schwaber, E. A. (1998). The non-verbal dimension in psychoanalysis: "state" and its clinical vicissitudes. *International Journal of Psychoanalysis, 79*: 667–677.

Segal, H. (1986). *The Work of Hanna Segal: A Kleinian Approach to Clinical Practice*. London: Free Association.

Segal, H. (1991). *Dream, Phantasy and Art*. London: Routledge.

Sherborne, V. (1990), *Developmental Movement for Children*. Cambridge: Cambridge University Press.

Soth, M. (2002). What is "working with the body"? *The European Journal of Psychotherapy, Counselling and Health, 5*(2): 121–133.

Sowa, A. (2002–2003). Sustained thinking and the realm of the aesthetic in psychoanalytic observation. *International Journal of Infant Observation, 5*(3): 24–39.

Stamenov, M. I., & Gallese, V. (Eds.) (2003). *Mirror Neurons and the Evolution of Brain and Language*. Amsterdam: John Benjamin.

Stanton, K. (1992). Imagery and metaphor in Group Dance Movement Therapy: a psychiatric outpatient setting. In: H. Payne (Ed.), *Dance Movement Therapy: Theory and Practice* (pp. 123–140). London: Routledge.

Steiner, J. (1993). *Psychic Retreats*. London: Routledge.

Stern, D. (1985). *The Interpersonal World of the Infant*. London: Karnac.

Stern, D. (2004). *The Present Moment in Psychotherapy and Everyday Life*. New York: W. W. Norton.

Symington, N. (1994). *Emotion and Spirit*. London: Cassell.

Toporkov, V. O. (1979). *Stanislavski in Rehearsal*. New York: Routledge.

Totton, N. (1998). *The Water in the Glass*. London: Rebus.

Totton, N. (Ed.) (2005). *New Dimensions in Body Psychotherapy*. London: Open University Press.

Tracey, N. (2000). Thinking about and working with depressed mothers in the early months of their infant's life. *Journal of Child Psychotherapy*, 26(2): 183–205.

Trevarthen, C. (1993). The functions of emotions in early infant communication and development. In: J. Nadel & L. Camaioni (Eds.), *New Perspectives in Early Communicative Development* (pp. 48–81). London: Routledge.

Trevarthen, C. (2004). Intimate contact from birth. In: K. White (Ed.), *Touch: Attachment and the Body* (pp 1–16). London: Karnac.

Turp, M. (2001), *Psychosomatic Health*. London: Palgrave.

Tustin, F. (1986). *Autistic Barriers in Neurotic Patients*. London: Karnac.

Tustin, F. (1990). *The Protective Shell in Children and Adults*. London: Karnac.

Urwin, C. (2002). A psychoanalytic approach to language delay: when autistic isn't necessarily autism. *Journal of Child Psychotherapy*, 28(1): 73–93.

Winnicott, D. W. (1945). Primitive emotional development. In: *Collected Papers: Through Paediatrics to Psycho-Analysis*. London: Tavistock, 1958.

Winnicott, D. W. (1949). Mind and its relation to the psyche-soma. In: *Collected Papers: Through Paediatrics to Psychoanalysis*. London: Tavistock, 1958.

Winnicott, D. W. (1960). Ego distortion in terms of true and false self. In: *The Maturational Processes and the Facilitating Environment* (pp. 140–152). London: Hogarth, 1972.

Winnicott, D. W. (1971). *Playing and Reality*. London: Tavistock.

Winnicott, D. W. (1988). *Human Nature*. London: Free Association.

Winston, R. (2003). *The Human Mind*. BBC television series.

Woolf, P. H. (1965). The development of attention in young infants. In: L. J. Stone, H. T. Smith, & L. B. Murphy (Eds.), *The Competent Infant: Research and Commentary*. London: Tavistock, 1974.

# INDEX